30119 018 900 383

LONDON BOROUGH OF SUTTON

WA.

40p

WATERSTEPS
ROUND EUROPE

**This book is to be returned on or before
the last date stamped below.**

22 JUL 1998

-7 NOV 2000

1 9 FEB 1999

13.4.99 MB

LONDON BOR.
WITHDRAWN
LIBRARIES & HERIT

SUTTON LEISURE SERVICES

SW6 0HY
081-770 4900

RENEWALS   Please quote:
            date of return, your ticket number and
            computer label number for each item.

D0840988

Other titles by the same authors:

Watersteps Through France: To the Camargue by Canal
ISBN 0 7136 4391 9

This book precedes *Watersteps Round Europe* and is the story of the
Coopers' trip in *Hosanna*, their seaworthy but half-finished Dutch barge
through the canals and rivers of France. Climbing the watersteps of the
Massif Central, they passed through some out-of-the-way places, made a
wonderful variety of friends, and had a great many adventures before
they arrived in time for Christmas in the peace and warmth of the
Camargue.

Sell Up and Sail 2nd edition
ISBN 0 7136 3948 2

This bestselling book is packed with first hand advice for anyone seeking
to escape from the rat race and take to a life at sea. Considered the bible
for longterm cruisers, it tells you everything you need to know – from the
practicalities and pitfalls of early retirement, choosing a boat to live in,
looking after her on the move, and organising your finances to prevent-
ing ill health afloat, choosing suitable cruising grounds, provisioning in
far flung places and deep sea voyaging.

Sail into the Sunset
ISBN 0 7136 3951 2

Sailors in their later years generally have very different requirements
from their younger counterparts, as Bill and Laurel Cooper have discovered during their travels around Europe aboard their Dutch sailing barge.
Covering every kind of boating from messing about in a dinghy on a
reservoir to boating on canals, chartering, racing and retiring to live
aboard, Bill and Laurel Cooper have drawn on their own experience to
provide a wealth of practical information and advice for people sailing in
their retirement.

SUTTON LIBRARIES
AND HERITAGE SERVICES
018 400 383
MAY 1998
914
95

WATERSTEPS
ROUND EUROPE

From Greece to England by Barge

BILL AND LAUREL COOPER

Adlard Coles Nautical
LONDON

Published 1996 by Adlard Coles Nautical
an imprint of A & C Black (Publishers) Ltd
35 Bedford Row, London WC1R 4JH

Copyright © Bill and Laurel Cooper 1996
Illustration copyright © Laurel Cooper 1996

The authors assert their moral rights.

ISBN 0-7136-4399-4

All rights reserved. No part of this publication may be
reproduced in any form or by any means – graphic,
electronic or mechanical, including photocopying,
recording, taping or information storage and retrieval
systems – without prior permission in writing of
the publishers.

A CIP catalogue record for this book is available from
the British Library.

Typeset in 10H on 12Hpt Sabon
Printed and bound in Great Britain by
The Cromwell Press, Broughton Gifford,
Melksham, Wiltshire

CONTENTS

ILLUSTRATIONS

INTRODUCTION

Hosanna is an elderly Dutch barge, almost the same age as we her owners, which gives us a certain sympathy and tolerance towards her. She has, like us, finished working for a living, and we have converted her into our floating and only home, a very mobile one.

She is comfortable, about the size inside of a small cottage with a living room (saloon) some 6m x 3m, two bedrooms each with own bathroom, a small but efficient kitchen (we are not much given to nautical jargon when more common terms will do just as well), and a workroom/studio. There are most of the other attributes of home. We have a cupboard under the stairs to keep the tennis racquets in (only it's not under the stairs), an attic (which is under the floorboards, as is the capacious cellar). We even have the equivalent of a garden shed in what sailors call the forepeak.

Above decks there is a verandah on which Laurel has a small herb garden and a few pots of geraniums. Bill escapes the tyranny of mowing a lawn, which may be the reason he enjoys living afloat: he is not pastoral by nature and has a black thumb. Water comes when we turn on a tap; but unlike most homes on land we have to fill the 5000 litre tanks at regular intervals, and this operation combines with washing down the boat, when local laws allow, which is a far more exhausting business than washing a car. Lights come on if the batteries are in good order, and the generator sees to that and the running of more powerful electrical devices.

What you step into as you leave the boat depends on where you moored the night before. It varies from parklike lawns and flower beds through well tended quays at deck level to concrete silo wharfs three metres above you, and from canalside fields and woods to unwelcoming shallows with toothy piles, where only the presence of bollards on a crumbling wall suggests a mooring at all. It can be a quiet spot in the country, with only the wind in the leaves and nightingales to disturb your sleep. If you were unlucky you could be next to a roaring motorway where the sodium lamps shine into the skylight all night, worse than a full moon. We try to avoid such moorings, but we cannot always choose.

Unlike cottagers, unless they run their own generators and pumping stations, we also have the engine room, which is a source of pride, power, and an inventive lexicon of imprecations; and a wheelhouse to ensure that the power engendered takes us to the right place. To help us do this (apart from the engine controls and steering position), we have, like most cruising boats nowadays, radar, echosounders, a Navtex weather recorder, and GPS (Global Positioning System) which makes navigation much easier than it was in the old days, though we still use the old ways to check that the new ones are not misleading us.

It is a rare day in *Hosanna* when everything works, but with back-ups, ingenuity, and dogged determination we usually arrive at our destination.

This time, we didn't.

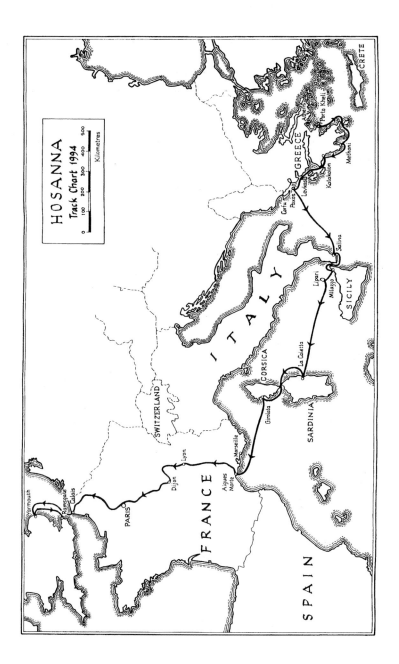

HOSANNA
Track Chart 1994

Kilometres
0 100 200 300 400 500

CRETE

GREECE
Athens
Porto Kheli
Methoni
Kalokolon
Levkas
Paxos
Corfu

ITALY

Salina
Lipari
Milazzo
SICILY

La Caletta
CORSICA
Girolata
SARDINIA

SWITZERLAND

Marseille
Lyon
Dijon
Aigues
Morte

FRANCE

Yarmouth
Ramsgate
Calais
PARIS

SPAIN

· 1 ·

WINTER QUARTERS

In which we lay plans and eat lotuses – the Moldavian
Tornado does his worst – we renew a source of power –
Greek dentistry – and untangle the winter web

'If we're going to get to England by summer' said the
Captain in February, 'we ought to set sail soon'.
We had said this before, several times. About once a week
since Christmas, in fact. There were good reasons to go back
to England: we wanted a new main engine since the present
one was giving us trouble; the generator needed replacing, and
we had provisionally booked to slip in Great Yarmouth in late
June. If we allowed a generous month for the work to be done,
we would have plenty of time to tart *Hosanna* up again (work
in boatyards always leaves one very dirty) and we could cruise
gently down to the South Coast, with maybe a stop in the
Medway to visit our son Ben in Rochester on the way. We
thought of joining in a Club Rally at Beaulieu in September,
and were definitely going to the Southampton Boat Show
where our next book was to be launched. It all fitted in rather
well.

But in Porto Xeli on the coast of Argolis in Greece, a good
dry spell was tempting us to paint ship, and then of course we
would deserve a rest to enjoy the sheer lotus-eating atmosphere of springtime Greece with the growing warmth of the
sun glancing off blue water and the cheapness of the wine at
Manoli's taverna, and should we not wait for Laurel's birthday
at the beginning of March and have a farewell quayside barbecue with the other boats whose denizens had been our
winter companions; and then what about Easter?

We dallied. If painting a boat can be called dallying. Left to ourselves it would have been a leisurely business, since we are not given to self punishment, but among the friends we had made that winter was a young Moldavian, Andreu, who was keen to work, and since we were keen to paint while the dry spell lasted, a bargain was struck. Andreu worked in a fashion we found completely exhausting since he had to be taught to use the equipment and materials, and supervising him was rather like running an eager ferret for nine hours a day. He worked for dollars, which would be sent home to his mother in Kishinev. One dollar a week keeps her comfortably, he said.

We believed him, having the summer before met yachts back from Odessa reporting that our penny was not a small enough coin for the markets of the Ukraine where if a commodity, such as potatoes, was available to the masses at all, a farthing would buy all you needed for a month. Andreu had in fact set sail from Odessa with eighty kilos of potatoes on board and very little else in the way of food. He rarely entered the Greek supermarkets, which we found so basic and simple, in spite of their proud boast outside of SUPEPMARKET. They were still like the old village shops of our childhood but with an added chest freezer leaking pink and watery pools of chicken juice. Andreu found the supermarkets a great culture shock and dreadfully expensive.

Andreu ought to have been a Hero of the Soviet Union. A Stakhanovite. Once pointed at a task, he would not stop until it was well finished.

'Andreu!' we would call out, 'Coffee break!'

'Why?' he would reply sternly. He would not join us. Worse, his disapproval made us feel guilty. For the first few days we gulped down our elevenses and hastened back to the task; then fortunately remembered that at our age life is not meant to be a penance, and reverted to our sloppy ways again. We could not keep up. We pleaded old age and infirmity and let him work at his own incredible pace. His curiosity and love of language were the only two things that would stop the work of the Moldavian Tornado, either to query a new English word, or learn a new technique. He watched Laurel bathing some corroded steel in ortho-phosphoric acid.

'What are you doing?' he asked.

'I am turning loose iron oxide into a hardened form of black iron phosphate that inhibits further rusting, and forms a key for chlorinated rubber paint,' she replied. Not that she is a chemist. But if you look after a boat you gather all kinds of knowledge, and that page in the *Steel Ship Painter's Manual* was one she knew well. Andreu watched her carefully for a moment.

'Such technology!' he said at last.

Andreu had in fact built his own small GRP yacht in Moldavia over about ten years, picking up bits of stainless steel and aluminium for rigging and fittings from scrapheaps by the local factory. He had used plans he had seen in a western magazine, and had adapted them to cope with the various materials discarded by the nearby armament factory. He had endured the hostility of authority. Anyone doing anything different from normal was suspect. Twice they had tried to have his boat destroyed, until at last came Perestroika, and officials were more occupied in worrying about their jobs than hounding young men building boats. Even so, he had had great difficulty getting an exit visa, and apparently this is one of the major problems with visiting the Ukraine: they are unwilling to let you go because the officials might possibly get into trouble for doing so and then they would not be able to undo the damage. If they get into trouble for keeping you there, that is a fault easily remedied.

So Andreu wore us out, working all daylight hours (although at first he arrived too early in the morning, and had to be persuaded that nothing could be painted till the dew was dry). The painting was advancing well, as he stacked up his one-dollar bills. Our bankers had been taken aback by our request for a fair amount of dollars in small denominations. They suspected some small scale money-laundering no doubt, but we explained about Russia and they were reassured. They were prepared to believe anything about Russia, and it was no use talking about the Ukraine, let alone Moldavia. These countries were not yet in the commercial vocabulary. One dollar was such a large amount to a modest family in the Moldavian countryside that it was impossible conveniently to exchange even a five dollar bill for the roubles needed for everyday living. So we paid him in bundles of 'oncers'.

What was of interest to us was that he was an example of a fairly common feature of our own culture, a man with sea mania. We have noted that these exist in all communities, whether or not there is any nautical tradition, or even a sea coast (Ukrainian Moldavia is landlocked and Andreu had to launch his boat in Odessa). It is a sort of infection that can spread in a community and it knows no frontiers. Such people have to go to sea, preferably in their own boat, no matter what sacrifices they might have to make. They do no real harm except to their own pockets, and for that reason the politicians are bound one day to interfere. Whenever things go wrong, the populists stone the eccentrics.

At night, after work, Andreu was excellent company. He ceased to be the tornado and became a waft of fresh air. He could sing and play on his guitar the complete works of the Beatles (indeed that was how he had learnt English), and over at Manoli's taverna with the other wintering yachties would also charm our ears with Russian songs. Some of the tunes we could join in with what we hoped were Cossack-like whoops and clapping. In return, we taught him sea shanties.

Apart from the delays caused by the painting, a repair to our generator was also holding us up. As shore power was not available at Porto Xeli, the recent lack of a generator had been irritating, but not as disastrous as if we had been in Northern climes. Our wood fire kept us warm in the evenings which was the only time we needed warmth most days, and Laurel cooked on her two gas rings, doing without the oven. We ran our noisy little spare generator as little as possible and had to make profuse apologies to our neighbours on *Peregrin, Two Lisas,* and *Hai Kung Chu.*

So it was with delight that we saw Dionysos's van coming along the quay with our generator, newly rewound. We man-handled the beast down into the engine room where it was reinstalled. In the delightful fashion that Greeks have, when they are not irritating you beyond belief, Dionysos also brought us a huge bag of oranges from his garden and six newlaid eggs. The oranges were the best we'd ever tasted: juicy, strongly flavoured, not too sweet and not too sour. Perfection is rare, and not to be expected, but when its benison touches you, it deserves celebration. Plus, we now had power back, which meant hot water and baking and a profligacy of light.

What were we waiting for now? The mail, as always. We decided that the hundred and one things that needed to be done after four months in one place would not take long, and that we could be away in a few days – as soon as the mail came, in fact. In the last week of February we cleaned and

returned the borrowed pontoon that had helped us paint the ship. Bill replaced damaged furling gear on the mizzen staysail. The vet came and gave both cats their annual anti-rabies shots. Laurel put away the breakable ornaments that come out of hiding when we settle, to return to safety in tissue paper and bubble plastic as she stowed the boat for sea. We got our hair cut. We stored ship: not hard in a place where the shops are on the quay fifty metres away and what they have not got, you have long ceased to worry about. We varnished the exterior objects that required it: the cuddy skylight and the ensign staff.

We had the farewell barbecue, an enjoyable affair in spite of non-cooperation by the weather which chose to send us the coldest wind of the winter as a last rude epithet before giving way to spring. Tuesday 1 March was Laurel's birthday. We celebrated by going out to the Rosas Taverna for dinner, where Laurel lost a back filling, unfairly she thought, as it was Bill who had the lively grilled lamb chops, which in Greece are always good exercise for the teeth and jaws. Laurel would have preferred to lose a filling over something more challenging than grilled sole. At our age, you get these things seen to, especially if you are going to be at sea shortly; so we sighed and prepared to lose a few more days. One has to take time to ask around one's friends to find a good dentist in any country. In any case, we were still waiting for the mail.

On Thursday we borrowed a car and drove to the metropolis seven kilometres up the hill, where Laurel's filling was restored by an impressive woman who owned a sterilizer and used gloves, which luxuries are not universally available the further east you go. On Friday Laurel cleaned and washed all twenty four of the paintbrushes we had used, and stowed the remaining paint tins back in the forepeak. The mail arrived. On Saturday the water tanker came, and we filled our tanks and washed the ship from end to end. Bill dismantled the wooden screens which protect the verandah in winter, and stowed them in the forepeak, replacing them with the roll-up canvas ones we use until high summer makes them unnecessary.

On Sunday morning early, before the breeze got up, we began to disentangle *Hosanna* from her winter cocoon. We had many offers of help, but had declined them; we like to do things at our own pace, and have a certain pride in coping alone. We had spent four months bows to the quay, with a huge tractor tyre to take the rub, and three anchors out.

The tyre came in first, too heavy to lift, but using the spar on our foremast as a derrick made it easier. After a last check that both cats were on board (this is usually achieved by delaying their breakfast until we have left the quay) we brought in the brow and stowed it, and cast off the two bow moorings. Next, as we left the quay the stern anchor, our biggest, came

Laurel.

7

in by hydraulic power, with a stop every metre for four months of mud and shellfish to be cleaned off with a wire brush. The last thirty metres of it required Laurel to be down below, stowing the cable so that it did not jam next time it was used. We then hauled in the sheet anchor, an extra one we had laid out on rope, also encrusted with months of maritime grot. Finally we got in the bower anchor, in Laurel's view the easiest one, perhaps because it was the one she used continuously and felt at home with.

All this had brought on board a great deal of mud, water, slime, and an intriguing mosaic of algae, knotted string, broken shells, fishhooks and rubber objects into which it did not do to look too closely, so we washed down anew, while we motored gently to the anchorage not far off shore and let the bower anchor go again. We had a bit more cleaning and stowing of ropes and anchors to do, and then lowered the dinghy, which is also done by means of the fore derrick, cleaned and tidied ourselves, and rowed ashore. It was noon. The hard work was done and we could join the other yachties for a last liquid Sunday lunch at Manoli's taverna.

Whatever Manoli offered in the way of ambience and refreshment, his establishment was not sophisticated. The décor would have seemed shabby even for a garden shed, but on fine winter Sundays we all sat outside on the quay, where it was much warmer. Manoli would not light the stove for us inside, even on very cold days, neither would he bring out the chairs and tables, as it was not summertime. So we brought them out ourselves, and he would follow, ts'sking as he wiped off the tin tables the dust which the cruel sun revealed, and brought out beer and jugs of wine (the cheapest and best in the district), the plates of chips (the best in Greece, his customers said) and, for those who were feeling expansive, a plate of those intensely Mediterranean-tasting fried fish, *maridaki*. The lemons that came with it were the size of melons. If you skipped the fish, you could eat and drink from noon till teatime for about 80p, in company with the best story-tellers in the world: sailors of both sexes and all nationalities.

We would miss them all, we said, as in mid-afternoon we bade them farewell, *au revoir, auf weidersehn, andio, da svedanya*, *arriverderci* and *tot ziens*; and rowed back to our boat, swinging at anchor.

We rowed in once more the following morning to pay our harbour dues, since the office had been closed on Sunday. This astonished the harbour authorities. 'You should have gone yesterday when we were not here!' they said, laughing at our innocence. We were rewarded though: one more packet of mail was waiting for us at the post office, and we bought one more freshly baked loaf before rowing back and hoisting in the dinghy. With the usual surge of hope and access of freedom that accompanies being stored up and ready for a long voyage, tanks topped, frig full, fragile belongings well stowed, the sofa and table screwed down, and a good weather forecast, we weighed anchor and set off on our 2300 mile journey back to England, two days after the feast of St Gerasimos (Minor Mental Disorders).

· 2 ·

IONIAN INTERLUDE

The Spring openeth the seas for sailors (PLINY)

In which Capes are passed – our sea monster stirs –
Ulysses' island – bad weather and good wine – we wait
for the omens

We passed Cape Matapan in the middle of the night of Monday, 7 March.

The day before we had emerged from the great bay where we had wintered, heading east-about round the island of Spetsai, and then turning south. The day had been fine, the sun sparkling on the waves, there was no wind to speak of, and only a gentle south-easterly swell lulled *Hosanna* into the open sea. Perfect weather for the start of a voyage. We had decided to go the long way round the south of Greece rather than go through the Corinth Canal, which would have been much shorter in distance, because the Greeks run the canal rather as British Rail run the railways. The less it was used, the higher they fixed their canal dues, until by 1994 the charge for using it had reached such a level that it would have provided most of the fuel we would use on our entire journey the long way round the Peloponnese. Eventually, one boat per year will use the short cut and be charged a million pounds for doing so. It won't be us.

At dusk, about half past six, we had passed Cape Malea, the first of the three fingers of the Peloponnesus, which point south-east to Crete. We turned west, to pass north of the island of Kithera. We switched on the radar and our navigation lights and prepared for the night, which, without the Night Box (in fact a wicker basket containing chocolate bars, nuts, raisins and apples) can seem very much too long, with only two of us to share the dark hours. The cats are no good at steering.

10

During the night we keep watches in turn, two hours at a time, the one off-watch sleeping out on the verandah on a lounging chair if the weather is warm, or as then when it was distinctly cool, on the wheelhouse bench wrapped in a sleeping bag, with the grey cat Bograt snoozing on their chest as catwaterbottle and comforter. The other cat, striped Tansy with white bib and socks, has no faith in us at all, and goes forward to the lifeboat when the engine starts, and remains there until the voyage is over: that is to say until the anchor cable rattles out through the hawsepipe, or we moor to a quay.

The watchkeeper sits centrally, facing the wheel and compass, with the radar and engine controls to the right, and with a big chart table and the GPS (Global Positioning System) instrument to the left.

Bill was on watch when we doubled Cape Matapan, which was right, as he has a sentimental feel for this Cape, the scene of one of the Royal Navy's major battles, one that kept the Italian Navy out of the rest of the last war. He noted with annoyance that the Hydrographer of the Navy had, for no good reason, changed its name on the chart to Akra Teneiron, thus showing a lack of respect by the non-combatants for the fighting part of the Navy. But he had no time to be worrying about it as we rounded. This was the most southerly point of our whole journey back to England. It is also a dangerous corner on a major shipping route to the east, as ships kiss the tips of the Peloponnesian fingers to save time and fuel, and a careful watch was needed. Often the lights of five or six ships were in plain sight ahead in the starlight and others were showing further away on radar.

Just after seven in the morning, Laurel watched the sun rise, her favourite night watch, and the ship's day began with a good breakfast for everyone except Tansy, who could not be found. The Navtex was consulted for the day's weather but nothing appeared on it. Laurel checked her weather log for last year and found she had recorded a similar blank in this area. We hoped the signal would come in again as we neared Kerkyra (Corfu), the next emitting station; meanwhile the sky held no threat, and the day was fine.

We also checked our position by GPS. This yankee device is a glorious boon. For years Bill relished being an old-fashioned navigator doing things the eye-ball way with sextants, bearing compasses, lead-lines and so on, and he has only recently bitten the electronic bullet. Now we cannot imagine how we managed before the days of milliamps. The instrument reads signals from several satellites and displays one's latitude and longitude with great accuracy, even allowing for the fact that Uncle Sam, in an uncharacteristic fit of meanness, has introduced a random error into the signals so that only his own ships can get the hyper-accurate data by using a secret decoder, and we lesser mortals must be content with a degree of accuracy that a few years ago would have been unimaginable.

Even this down-graded version is too accurate for the British Admiralty charts of Greece. Many of these were surveyed by a Captain Mansell in 1864, and the best one can say about him is that he was no Captain Cook. The result is that when coasting, any positions taken off the GPS receiver and plotted on the chart are likely to indicate that one is engaged in mountain climbing rather than sailing. It is very disturbing to transfer one's latitude and longitude to the chart and find that *Hosanna* is apparently halfway up the crag that beetles over the anchorage. Of course the electronics are correct, but it does make navigation a little more trying not to know the latitude and longitude of perilous portions of coastline as drawn on the chart, and a second data provider is desirable. We have eyes, and use them. We also have radar, which gives our position relative to the land at night, or in bad visibility. The depthsounder is also a check if you are in soundings.

If the Hydrographer of the Navy would correct his charts, he would save us all a lot of anxiety, as well as enhance his own considerable reputation, but two factors inhibit him from doing so. The Greek government forbids foreigners from carrying out any surveys of their coast, but fails to do anything effective about it themselves. This would not inhibit the Hydrographer normally, for passing ships of many types (including *Hosanna*), take observations surreptitiously and send him the results, but sadly, the British government of a few years ago acquired an enthusiasm for metrication, and most of the resources of the Admiralty were devoted to changing the units on thousands of charts (a process that is still only about half completed) at enormous expense while leaving many navigators to cope with out-of-date charts that are not compatible with modern navigational aids. Metrication kills!

During the morning a noise in the engine which had perturbed us during the night became a little worse, and a choppy sea got up, stirred by a wind from quite the wrong direction. This was enough to decide us to pause at Methoni.

We had accomplished a respectable 135 miles as we passed the familiar but always breathtaking Turkish Tower on the point at Methoni, and slid behind the breakwater, dropping anchor under the Venetian fort. Whenever we anchor here, we feel the breath of history, we see the merchant galleys of Venice, smell the spices they carry, and hear the crack of Ottoman cannon.

Reality intervened. When all was quiet but the lapping water and the sound of the rising wind (we had been wise to pause) Tansy revealed her presence in the gas bottle locker, where she had made a comfortable nest, but would now like breakfast, thank you very much.

For a couple of days we waited at Methoni, watching a heavy swell breaking in high flung spray on the harbour bar. Bill suspected that our fuel oil, which had lain in our tanks over the winter, might have become contaminated and he changed the filters and did some topping up that he hoped would improve the engine. Laurel made bread and baked a quiche. We bent on the two sails that we had not had leisure to do before. As we hoped, the Navtex weather from Kerkyra had come in as we rounded the last cape, so we now knew that the wind was expected to decrease.

Suddenly it dawned on us that in the first few days of our journey we had spent only two days actually travelling, and two sheltering, and that if we continued thus it would take twice as long to get to England. A bit more urgency was required.

However in the end we set sail a bit too soon, though the breakers on the bar had subsided and the wind seemed much less threatening. We spent an uncomfortable day heading north with the wind against us, and towards afternoon had to reduce speed as the waves rose. The sight of a school of dolphins, our first for the year, comforted us for the racing screw and the spray coming over the bows as we pitched into a choppy sea. After sunset, having done 55 miles, we tired of it and headed into Katakolon for a night's rest, berthing alongside at nine o' clock (at least in March there was plenty of room, despite a number of large fishing boats in for the weekend). We made a beeline for fish and chips at Jason's *estiatorion* close by; a mecca for the lover of Greek fish and chips, even out of season. Especially out of season. We invaded the kitchen to pay our respects to Mama, and ate inside the small crowded room with its windows steamed up and running with condensation, while the TV relayed yet another Greek politician trying to look and sound convincing and sincere.

It was still dark when we left next morning before daybreak, collecting Tansy off the quay where she was having words with a seagull, and made the 65 miles to Ithaka just before dark, anchoring off the old short pier, where Bill had anchored

14

41 years before to lend assistance after the earthquake, and where we had since come many times, formerly with *Fare Well* and latterly with *Hosanna*.

Even in a hurry we had time to enjoy the particular feeling of coming again to Ithaka, kingdom of Odysseus/Ulysses, that great cheeky wanderer and teller of tall tales. Even in a hurry we never forgot the words of Cavafy which we were beginning to have years enough to fulfil:

> *Be quite old when you anchor at the island,*
> *Rich with all you have gained on the way,*
> *Not expecting Ithaka to give you riches.*
> *Ithaka has given you your lovely journey.*
> *Without Ithaka you would not have set out.*
> *Ithaka has no more to give you now.*

We launched the dinghy and rowed ashore for Saturday night *kokkoretsi* (a kebab of spiced lamb's innards unbeloved by most Europeans but relished by the Ionians, and Bill) and lamb chops at the 'Three Ks' where friendly fishermen shared a plate of dateshells with us, a great honour because they are highly prized. These are called *lithophages* in zoological Greek: stone-eaters, because they drill into limestone, forming a perfectly shaped hole for themselves. Most European languages call them dateshells, since they are lookalikes for their shape, size, and warm brown colour.

The fishermen reminded us that tomorrow was Carnival Sunday, the last day before Lent, and that we *had* to stay for Carnival. Well, of course.

Lent in the Ionian Islands is pretty grim for the Orthodox believer. The last two Sundays before Lent begins are 'Meat Sunday' and 'Cheese Sunday'. These and other commodities are used up, with a last feast on Carnival, because it is not just meat that is being waved goodbye. For more than forty days (since Greek Lent begins on Monday, not Ash Wednesday) the islanders will not eat meat, cheese, milk, oil or eggs. The strictest of them will live on bread and water, beans, green herbs, and *halva*, a sweet made of semolina and almonds, probably the only thing that makes it possible to persevere with this rigorous diet.

After forty days of that, how welcome is the roasting smell of the Easter lamb. We, alas, would not be in Greece to share the lamb: Orthodox Easter was very late that year, almost the end of April, and we were hoping to be well on our way by then.

Meanwhile Carnival on Ithaka was all that an island carnival should be, the prettiest girl chosen as Queen, and dignified with a donkey cart, and the Town Accountant disguised, rather well we thought, as a dustbin. When we rowed back to *Hosanna* afterwards there were streamers and confetti on the bottomboards of the dinghy.

The morrow was Clean Monday, the first day of Lent, when everyone flies kites. We flew only our ensign as we left Ithaka, northbound for Levkas. It was only thirty miles, and we arrived just after lunch.

After two years in Greek seas we had decided to come back to England for two main reasons: the first was to replace the main engine that was virtually worn out, preferably before it let us down, and the second was to sample a little home waters sailing that we had not experienced for over twenty years of wandering the seas of the world.

We found ourselves between two intractable parameters. Winter navigation in the Mediterranean is as perilous as winter navigation in more northern waters. In classical times sailing was forbidden in Greek winters, and all boats were hauled out on to the beach in the winter months. With on the one hand a big boat, and on the other a small crew, we had felt that we could perhaps start the local, coastal part of our voyage in March, provided we waited carefully for a good weather forecast, and chose our sailing times with care.

The longer parts of the voyage, however, crossing the Ionian Sea for example, where we would be more than 24 hours from any shelter if the capricious spring weather decided to change, were quite another matter. After a week of travelling we were now well up the Ionian coast of Greece, having sailed a good deal of it inside the protecting islands, but would soon have to make the long jump to Italy, and the weather had not yet settled.

The other end of the voyage was equally limiting, because the time booked on the slipway in July, and the boat show obligation in September, were a sort of deadline. The longer we stayed in Greece, the more we would have to get a move on, and we do not like to cruise in too much of a hurry. It was becoming painfully apparent that to have a leisurely voyage home we should already have left Greece, westward bound; there were after all over two thousand miles to go. Perhaps we should have paid more attention to this at the outset, but ours is usually a relaxed way of life; we are not in the habit of looking ahead too far, so we feel we might be forgiven for our somewhat leisurely start.

The feeling of impatience was unwelcome. We retired early specifically to avoid such life-destroying pressures as a sense of urgency. We were breaking a cardinal rule of life by being in a hurry. We had extracted ourselves from our winter quarters, had sailed round the three southern finger-tips of the Peloponnessus, and had arrived in the Ionian, which we knew well, and among whose islands we had many friends. Now, despite our best intentions and the need to get on, the voyage went onto hold for a bit, for reasons that are not totally clear to us, but probably have more to do with a love of Greek islands and a resistance to speed than to feeble excuses about the weather. The main engine had given signs of belligerence, and we had had a roughish passage up the west coast. Maybe our nerve was, if not lost, hidden at the bottom of the oilskin cupboard. In any event the after capstan needed repair, we told ourselves, and Laurel was starting a sore throat, which wanted cossetting.

Since it seemed we were to be in Levkas for a week or ten days, we quietened our conscience and gave our stay credibility by arranging for the proofs of the current book to be sent to us for checking, and while waiting for them to arrive we had a pleasantly social interlude visiting old friends, being visited, and meeting new friends. We took the chance to make some improvements in the galley, and resurface the top of the table that spends the summer in the verandah, where we take all our meals in warm weather. A major repair to the after capstan was effected, including surgery (removal of a chunk of metal that was impairing performance). The plants in Laurel's one square metre garden were refurbished or replaced.

It was nearly the end of March before the proofs arrived, and English Easter was upon us, causing a dreadful sense of dichotomy. Greekwise we were still in Lent, and in the small islands the butchers had closed their doors for a long lean break. It didn't seem right to be celebrating Easter when Lent had only just begun, just as it had also not seemed right in Porto Xeli to start Lent a month earlier than the Greeks. The problem was almost insoluble, but pragmatism intervened; if we did not have our Hot Cross Buns now we should miss them altogether, westward bound. In Levkas, being a megalopolis quite the size of Beccles, the butchers were not closed, and illicit delights were freely available. The fish was wonderful and cheap, and we had mourned the absence of it in Porto Xeli, where there was no fish shop, and any catch landed went straight to Athens.

There was a holiday atmosphere, as Levkas had already become very busy with visiting Easter yachtsmen whom we loved to talk to, so to avoid temptation and to gain uninterrupted working time when the proofs arrived, we went ten miles down the coast to Vlikho, an anchorage completely surrounded by hills, well protected, but close to the village of Nidri for supplies, and we buckled down to work. As light relief when computer collapse set in, Laurel had found a source of bitter oranges and was making marmalade. In the evenings we rowed ashore and met more old and new friends.

A week's work got the proofs done, but a system of strong gales was passing and kept us weatherbound for several days more, since the anchorage at Vlikho was a far better place to be in bad weather than the quay at Levkas, which could be dangerous in a southeasterly. Even so, we occasionally had to set an anchor watch at night. This means physically sitting up and keeping watch that the anchor does not drag. Which is a drag. It is one of the things that people who gush over our wonderful lifestyle don't think about. It is boring in a way that a watch at sea never is.

In the end it was not at night that the really bad squall came, but in mid-afternoon. Mercifully some prick of instinct after lunch had prompted us to get the dinghy hoisted in, since in a calm anchorage we often leave the dinghy alongside us so that someone can do a quick row ashore to dump the rubbish or to buy bread. We heard a growing roar as a violent wind came down the mountainside and struck the waters of the anchorage which roiled and hissed. Visibility became nil as white water spun off the surface into a turbulent fog as high as our masthead. The squall hit us broadside on with a slam that felt as if we had been run into by the Albert Hall doing eighty knots, which was the recorded wind speed. We heeled over to about thirty degrees, started to make leeway, and felt the anchor break out.

The next hour was the down side of cruising, the 1% that makes you wonder what the hell you're doing.

Laurel grabs her oilskin and slings it round her – no time to button it up.

Get the engines on.

Get the radar on so we can tell where the shore is: you can't see even a boat's length for spray.

Get the anchor in quickly – it's doing worse than no good. You can't manoeuvre out of trouble with 30 fathoms of cable hanging down below the boat, and in any event we will need the anchor ready to let go again.

From the forward anchor winch Laurel, holding on to our blessedly strong guardrails against the snatch of the wind, eyes almost shut against the water needles spearing her face, watches as the chain toils up, seeming to come in so slow, so slow. Every few feet it stops, going out almost horizontally before it enters the water, and our powerful hydraulic windlass cannot pull it in. Voices are useless in the roar of the wind; Bill is making Why so long? gestures, and Laurel can only throw up her hands and shrug. It takes as long as it takes. He tries to manoeuvre to take some of the strain off the cable, but as he cannot see which way it is pointing he is not very successful.

After a three hour battle which lasted ten minutes, Laurel signalled that the anchor was safely in. Bill beckoned her back to the wheelhouse, where the sudden absence of tearing wind and noise and wet and cold was almost as shocking as its presence.

'She's under control, and I can see on radar where we are. Have a towel. We'll jill about till it eases and then drop anchor again.'

As the wind slackened, and the water returned to its proper place, the land appeared again. We had as we thought been blown down towards the narrows leading to seaward. On a gentle slope to one side of the narrows were hundreds of little flotilla yachts, shored up on oildrums for the winter.

Had been. The dozen nearest the shore had been knocked down like skittles, their masts and rigging now at all angles like a game of spillikins; and some boats that had been launched ready for Easter had been blown across the bay and were stranded on the opposite shore.

We re-anchored in dead centre of the large bay, the wind having died, and dried ourselves, quietening our high adrenalin levels with cups of tea.

We dined aboard on asparagus and roast quail, with a bottle from our special cellar of vintage claret, a 1961 Château Batailley. It had, as Laurel said without rancour, been rather a funny way to spend our wedding anniversary.

Our friends and wine-buffs marvel between respect and contempt that we take our good wines travelling. 'Such wines should be kept still and cool, not disturbed etc etc', they tell us time and time again. We, for our part, point out that we have never yet opened a dud bottle, in spite of the wines having survived a hurricane at sea and countless storms. It is true that the 1961 Calon Ségur got a little thin and began to lose its colour, but we found that a sample that has lain in Bill's sister's cellar in ideal conditions had started to go the same way. The Batailley, the Montrose and the Ducru Beaucaillou have not. We think one can be a bit too fussy about these things which are, above all else, instruments of pleasure and not sacramental icons. We have them, not often because we cannot afford them often, but occasionally as a celebration, when it is a joy to be able to drink liquid silk.

After another day of gales we seized a lull and returned to Levkas to post the finished proofs to England and make final preparations for our departure. The weather pattern was still extremely unstable, and gave us time to restock our cupboards and resume a gay and social life. Because of the weather we went alongside, with our bows pointing south-east into the prevailing wind where we were safer than mooring bows to the quay as the port police often asked us to do if space was short; the Easter rush was over for the moment and there was room. We rose a day or two later to see heavy snow on the mountains to the north, we were told that some people had gone ski-ing, and the wind got up again. By midday the yachts moored bows to further to the south round the corner were very uncomfortable, with quite big waves and spray breaking over the quay and flooding the road, and we ended the day with four small yachts moored alongside us, two and two, at our invitation; not the first time we have acted as a windbreak for smaller vessels.

A day later the wind died, we lost our stable of little yachts, and there we were, farewells made, ready to go, waiting for Spiro to come and fuel us for the long journey. We were by now two weeks late. Spiro turned up a day late. We knew he would. He always does.

Seagoing on our terms denies us the opportunity to come and go as we please. We might be in what one could call a background hurry, but in the foreground it is necessary to compound with safety, and during the two weeks we spent in Levkas only a fool or a masochist would have set out over the Ionian Sea.

We snatched another lull in the weather to sail up to the northern tip of Paxos, and dropped anchor in Lakka Bay, a good jumping off place for Italy, and sat there waiting for fair winds and calm seas. It was the season for neither.

How Lakka has changed in twenty years! On our first visit many years ago, we had rowed ashore to the only small taverna, its windows steamed up on a cool October evening. The taverna was packed, but kindly souls moved up and made room, and we found ourselves in a corner contemplating the backs of the community. Swiftly given a plate of unidentifiable stew (which was probably *sofrito*, a Corfiot dish of veal and garlic), bread, and a bottle of retsina, we were then politely ignored. The taverna housed the only television set in the village (black and white, of course) and Greece was playing Scotland at soccer.

We could not see the screen, but it was not necessary. We could feel every action as the room swayed in unison with the movements of the game. At half time there was an explosion of noisy voices and the glug of glasses being replenished. The assembly turned from the TV and took proper note of us for the first time. Obviously we were the ENEMY.

No, we said, we are not Scottish. We are English. It was quite clear that these people felt it was the same thing. Nowadays we know Greece well and can speak the language a little, so we would be able to explain that it is like the difference between the Ionians and the Cretans, and they would understand. As things were, it was all ANGLIA to them. We encountered the same problem later when posting a letter to Wales. (We have never understood why we, coming from the most easterly point in the British Isles, should have our tax inspector resident in Llanishen near Cardiff. This is the sort of administrative logic that sent us abroad in the first place.) We had put OUALLIA on the envelope and the clerk had firmly added ANGLIA after it. It would not get there otherwise, he said, everyone knew that OUALLIA was in ANGLIA.

Like it or not, in the taverna we were now suspect, and prayed that in the second half no Scottish player would transgress the norms of decent football as interpreted by a very partisan crowd of Hellenes. The game ended in a draw, something not conducive either to Greek over-exuberance, or that deep Hellenic melancholy that is expressed as xenophobia. The guitar came down off the wall, and they sang songs, sad ones mostly, with great emotion and gusto.

Nowadays the old taverna has been replaced by a smart restaurant, and there were even fast food joints, most of which were not yet open. The disco was being redecorated, thank God. We bought meat, a very nice piece of fillet steak, some pork chops and *loukanika*, locally made sausages. We stocked up with fresh vegetables, two gallons of the superb Paxos olive oil, which is always sold by weight (bring your own containers) and fresh eggs, probably from the spouses of the cock that woke us early every morning. The weather stayed bad for several more days; no Kairos Aithrios.

At last those were the words we heard on the radio, translated into 'fine weather' by the young lady who re-read the nautical forecast in English, promising us the weather we sought. Her tones are very correct and formal, Bill wishes she would occasionally drop in a personal happy word for all those sailors who hang on her lips at 0630 each morning. The Navtex echoed her words on its little green screen.

We left early in the day, Tuesday 19 April, to accomplish the 300 miles to the Straits of Messina. It would be our longest sea passage on the journey to England.

· 3 ·

SICILIAN STRAITS

In which the monster strikes – we brave the Fibia – the
wild tides of Messina – Scylla and Charybdis – and the
lairs of the Mafia

As soon as we cleared the harbour we made sail with a brisk
favourable breeze blowing over a mildly choppy sea. It
was early in the morning, cool and with a heavy dew. We made
about five knots, a good walking speed, saving fuel and being
good little ecological souls. This never lasts long, unfortunately.
Batteries have to be charged, or machines run, or the wind
becomes unsuitable in strength or direction.

We ran with the main engine gently assisting the sails for the
whole day. Just after midnight the wind eased, so we increased
the revs, and then at 0100 the water pump on the Cummins
main engine failed. We continued on the little Perkins stand-by
engine, and then after breakfast Bill went down to the engine
room to try to sort out the pump problem.

He found that the main engine had more than just a pump
problem. When he tried to turn the engine over with the
starter, it had locked solid and there was evidently liquid in the
cylinders. Faced with two apparently separate difficulties to
solve in quite a choppy sea, he retired on deck once more for
a bit of thinking time. As we were making tolerably good
progress towards the straits with the sails assisted by the little
Perkins, he gave up for the time being. We made the decision
to try for a harbour short of the straits to see if something
could be done, but he was not altogether content, and as the
sea had started to ease in the afternoon he decided to have a
go at the engine.

24

One can get water in the cylinders in rough weather if sea water comes up the exhaust pipe; it hadn't been that rough, but it was the obvious hypothesis to test. Bill spent an uncomfortable hour or two down below in the heaving engine room screwing down valves until he found out which cylinder was full, and then turning the engine by hand until it had emptied. Then he readjusted the valves, and vroom! away she went at a full 6 knots, Bill tempering his bad temper with the satisfaction of success, a valuable sensation as he is not a trained engineer, and has merely accumulated some elementary knowledge through observation of those who are. But though he had overcome the problem of this dose of liquid in the cylinders, he had not managed to repair the water pump, and without cooling water he could not keep it going. We had to shut the main engine down and went on all night on the little Perkins and berthed in the harbour at Saline in time for breakfast.

During the forenoon Bill again attacked the Cummins. He found the cylinders again full and confirmed that the water was fresh by the expedient of tasting the beastly black and unappetising stuff. He thought this must be a blown head gasket. Nevertheless he ran an improvised cooling water circuit using a spare wash-down pump fed through a spaghetti junction of plastic piping, but wasn't able to test it. We carried a spare cylinder-head gasket, but the trouble was that the bolts needed a torque-wrench capable of exerting a force of 400 ft lbs, and such tools are rare.

We could go on using the little Perkins. It would give us only 40% of the speed the main engine could give, which would expose us to more than twice the risk of adverse weather changes, and because it had an off-centre prop it would make our progress sort of crab-like, but it would keep us going to search for a Cummins agent with a gargantuan torque-wrench.

We had reason to worry a bit, for this was the season of capricious weather and we had little idea how long the weather 'window' would last. We do not relish bad weather at sea at any time, and with our main source of power lost to us, the situation gave us concern.

The port of Saline is just under the big toe on the bottom of the foot of Italy. We were relieved to be there, after two and a half days at sea.

We have spent three winters in Italy, in widely differing areas, and got to know the country. Saline, in Calabria, is not one of our favourite spots, but we are occasionally glad it is there. It is an ugly bare harbour built to serve a large chemical factory, whose tall chimney makes a very good landmark from seaward. The harbour setting was empty and desertlike, with wide concrete expanses, some patches of scrub, a rusty railway line, and not a habitation in sight. The silent chemical works close by had never come on line: it was finished with all its bits and pieces, its office block, laboratory, tanks and silos, and then it was closed. It had been built with EEC money to provide work for the Mezzogiorno (the deprived south of Italy), but no one in Brussels had bothered to find out if there would be a market for its product, Dioxin, which was in any case now a banned substance. Streaks of rust were beginning to stain the silos.

A harbour had been specially built for merchant ships to bring in the raw materials and take away the finished product, and there it was, almost new, completely unused except for a few small fishing boats and the occasional passing yacht. There is no other safe haven along this stretch of coast. Whether the building of the harbour is due to an incompetent piece of bureaucracy or a competent piece of corruption is not clear, but it was useful to us. We speculated why the men behind corruption always seem more competent than the administrators. Would it be better to in the final balance to have corrupt leaders? The population would have the benefit of, say 90% of their achievements, and might do rather better that way than getting the 100% of the blessings of less able, honest men. Well, the people of the South of France, especially in Nice, seem to think so.

The harbour was well finished. The quay walls were so high, being built for large ships, that in *Hosanna* you could not see over them, and the cats could jump ashore only from the wheelhouse roof. They soon got bored with the concrete and came back. We decided that corruption was more likely to be behind the building of the harbour than bureaucracy, especially when a Mr Fixit appeared on a Vespa to see if he could do us for something. Such a man will either become your lifelong friend, or screw the gold from your back teeth. In the Mezzogiorno you are still in the Levant.

The Greeks say that if a cat licks herself with her face turned to the north, that is where the wind will blow from. Our voyage had been too fraught for us to notice the behaviour of our cats, but we had just made shelter in time. For several days it blew hard from the north west, just the direction we wanted to go. We were joined by Niki and Jamie in their small self-built yacht *Siandra* which they had sailed from Australia. They too were on their way to England. We found kindred souls in their attitude to the sea and cruising; so much in common in spite of a substantial difference in our ages. It is often like that at sea: differences of age, sex, class and nationality disappear behind the common ground of experience.

We had started to run low on fresh provisions, since the shops at Lakka had been very basic, and we fancied some of those special Italian delicacies that are not available in Greece. There is no town, village, or even settlement at Saline, the nearest centre is five kilometres away at Melito. Hence Mr Fixit. Having been caught before by bandits offering to get everything we wanted, and then slapping on a delivery charge that would have paid for the two of us to fly to Eurodisney, we declined his services.

Laurel's dislocated hip prevents her walking that far. She usually gets round the problem by sailing the dinghy in from an anchorage. Here in Saline Bill had to be trusted with the really skilled work of running a ship: victualling. He set off with a list, his Barclaycard, a book of Eurocheques, a passport (which in theory one no longer needs in EU countries, but which, in our experience, is these days more essential than ever), a shopping bag, and poor expectations. Halfway to the village he got a lift in a passing truck which saved his feet a little, and cheered him up.

There were only two banks in the town, and he selected the only one which displayed any sign of wanting to know foreigners. If there were any postcards at all outside the shops, they were of somewhere else, always an indication of the absence of any tourist activity whatsoever. He made a good beginning, finding for a start that he could not get into the bank. There was a sanitized air-lock through which one must pass, the outside door must be shut before the inside would open. Each time he tried to pass the second door buzzers sounded and all doors locked up solid. Security men arrived to release him, and searched him, testing every item that they removed. At last they tested his reading glasses, the buzzer went off again and all the doors locked solid once more. When all this had been resolved they let him in the bank, but would not allow him to take in his glasses. The security man stayed in the 'air-lock', holding the possibly lethal glasses in his fingertips as if they were about to explode. In vain Bill protested at the counter that he would have difficulty reading without them. Rules is rules! Nothing that sets off the buzzers is allowed in the bank. Wondering about people with pace-makers, he realised that in Calabria a bank is not a business dealing in money that needs some security. It is a security company that plays with money as a sideline.

No, of course they would not cash a Eurocheque. Yes, *daccordo*, there was a sign on the door in red, white and blue with letters *EC* on it, but that had been sent to them with the instructions to stick it on the door. No one knew why. Yes, they could permit him some Lira on his Barclaycard if he would wait while they telephoned Milano. The wait was surprisingly short and Bill was told he could have something with a huge amount of zeros after it, roughly equivalent to £100, which is rather less than the Barclaycard gentlemen in England lead one to expect will be immediately forthcoming on waving their magic little card about in foreign banks. Bill did not argue. The firmness with which his reading glasses had been withdrawn reminded him that it is unhealthy to discuss things with banks in *Fibia* country (the *Fibia* is the Calabrian equivalent of the Camorra in Naples, or the Mafia in Sicily) where the concept of the listening bank involves eavesdropping on rivals, and with any luck, shooting them. It would be enough cash to last a week or so, if we had no big expenditures on the boat.

Laurel.

He walked down the small street and bought bread, mussels, and fresh fish (the one doing the shopping gets to buy what they fancy) and then started the long walk back which would take him past the *supermercato* on the outskirts of town. Here he added tubes of tomato paste (in Greece only tins are available, which are wasteful), fresh pasta all'uovo and a substantial amount of ox-tail, his favourite meal.

It is, he feels, a form of meat product that should appeal to animal rights people as, strictly speaking, there is no necessity to kill the animal in order to eat it. He walked back along the side roads, enjoying the late spring warmth, and the open country with the strong wind blowing across it and out to sea.

We had a little party that night with Jamie and Niki, dining on fresh pasta al'uovo with mussels alla *Hosanna* and watching the weather programme on Italian TV. Our Navtex was no longer getting any messages, we were too far from Kerkyra, and the next weather station to come in would be Ostend, Lord love us. For the Western Mediterranean and the whole of France we now must rely on radio and TV for weather information. It appeared to be good news, the wind was going to ease up.

So the next day we left, timing our departure to suit the tides in the Straits of Messina. We were headed for Milazzo, through the Straits and round the corner on the Northern coast of Sicily.

Most people believe there are no tides in the Mediterranean because that is what they are taught at school, but they exist. Tides are in reality enormous long waves that follow the sun and moon round the earth, each wave taking roughly twelve hours to pass. The Mediterranean is effectively separated from the oceans, but is big enough to experience its own waves of tide. These are usually only about 20–30 cm in height, except in certain places like Venice, but the waves pass by at the same intervals of time.

The waves do not travel in the same direction everywhere. Around Sicily they travel from west to east. As the wave comes to the pointed western tip of Sicily it is divided. One part goes along the shorter northern coast until it reaches the northern end of the Straits of Messina. The other part has to travel two sides of this triangular island to get to the southern end of these short straits, and it arrives there later in time. We thus have the remarkable situation that a tidal difference in height of only a few centimetres can generate an enormous flow from one end of the Straits to the other because the height difference is over a very short horizontal distance. This phenomenon was well known to the ancients, because the force of water-flow produced the impressive whirlpools which were dangerous enough to the small ships of the day to engender the most fearful legends. The best known of these concerns the perils of passing in the narrows between two whirlpools: that of Charybdis near mid-channel, and that of Scylla, near the dangerous rocky promontory of the same name. (Scylla was personified as a sea monster with a band of barking dogs round her belly, and a taste for raw sailors, not totally dissimilar from the holiday village on the site today.) In those days it wasn't just the nice girls who loved a sailor. For supper.

Fortunately for us, Charybdis and its fellows are less strong than they used to be owing to the earthquake of 1783 which changed the contours of the bottom of the Straits, but they can still cause trouble to small craft especially at times of full moon, when the tidal streams are at their strongest.

We have been through the Straits many times and have always been careful to take measurements of the strength of the tide. The strongest we ever recorded was 5.6 knots, which speed, though of little concern for a modern motor-ship, was rather more than the 3.6 knots which was the maximum we could hope to achieve with our main engine unusable, and only our little wing engine to rely on. It was therefore essential to plan our transit to coincide with the northbound tide. Unfortunately the change in the direction of the tide comes down from the north, so that we would be going towards it, and thus would have less than the six hours to go through the Straits that we could have expected in theory. The Straits are about thirty miles long, and they narrow as you proceed towards the Northern, difficult, end. It would be a tight race against time, as once the tide turned we would be swept back towards our starting point again. Trepidation for breakfast.

The day was bright and clear, with a stunning view of distant Mount Etna, over there on Sicily, her snowcapped peak wreathed with a plume of smoke. James and Niki visited, and after discussing our strategy they opted to do the same and follow us to Milazzo, which was safely round the corner in Sicily.

In the end, in our anxiety, we started too early, just after one pm, and for a time made no progress at all, despite putting up two staysails to take advantage of a light south-easterly wind. The early start was an error in the right direction, or should we say it was an error in no direction at all (metaphors can sometimes be unhelpful); at all events Etna remained obstinately about the same distance behind us. Then the tidal stream became slack and we started to inch forward, but it was now 1700, and we were getting very anxious: teatime trepidation had set in. We had allowed for the tide being strongly with us till six pm, and if we were to get no benefit soon it would turn before we reached the top of the Straits and sweep us back to Saline. The ferries from Messina to Reggio and San Giovanni crossed and recrossed ahead of us, and we seemed to spend most of our time keeping out of their way.

Everything seemed to happen at the last minute. At six pm the current achieved its full north-flowing strength and we seemed to be flying along at an indecent speed, all of 7H knots, which gave us some excitement as we passed through the whirlpool of Charybdis and found ourselves suddenly slammed off course by 60° before we made it across the turbulent circle and passed into calmer water again. The waves in the whirlpool had the form of hundreds of pinnacles about 50 cm high, all moving in a fast flowing circle that was quite like the emptying plug-hole of a gigantic bath. At dead of a moonless night with a strong wind howling in the rigging, it would be easy to inhabit the Straits with monsters like Scylla. We, however, saw no ravening virago with an odd taste in belts. She has dwindled into the seaside resort on the mainland that bears her name, probably as a landlady.

The slack at the other end of the harmonic arrived at seven pm, when we were still a little short of rounding Cape Pelorus, the northern tip of the Straits. Fortunately we had a short period of slack water in which to make a dash, and then a couple of hundred yards to go as the tide turned against us.

It was close.

We just made the point at 1915 and headed away along the north coast of Sicily into a blood-red sunset. The rest of the

32

journey was easier. James and Niki had sometimes sailed past us and sometimes lagged behind with the vagaries of wind and current. Now, while we hugged a well known shore, they prudently stood off to sea. They were the wiser in the end; we spent most of the next few hours dodging in the dark in and out of small unlit fishing boats, who seemed to think we could hear what they were shouting.

We arrived at the little port of Milazzo in the small hours of the night, and even though we knew it well, had difficulty identifying lighthouses and buoys against a background of flashing neon signs. Convention should proscribe flashing coloured lights near the entrance to ports, especially in line with the approach channel. Mostly, today's ships have radar, and rely on the lights as back-up, but having been brought up the old-fashioned, prudent way, Bill likes to see where he is going. As ships cannot reasonably have headlights, their captains prefer only the important things ashore to be lit with flashing lights.

Siandra came in early the following morning, having waited till daylight to enter a harbour unknown to them (a most prudent action which impressed Bill greatly), and berthed alongside us.

Milazzo is about the only congenial port in this part of Sicily. The Italian Navy, together with the state-owned ferry companies, have made nearby Messina one of the least hospitable ports in the world, quite unnecessarily, as there is plenty of room for small craft if an effort were to be made to accommodate them.

We had stopped in order to get some advice, at the very least, and better still some practical help, on the subject of what to do with a six-cylinder diesel engine apparently eager to run on water instead of oil, and unsuccessful in this ambition. Who knows, if we could discover the secret of how to make it do what it seemed to be bent on doing, we would be rich.

The port of Milazzo is in process of being reconstructed, which makes it rather less congenial at the moment, but also made it free of charge, which motivates one to put up with the dirt and noise. On this occasion the dirt was still there but the noise had ceased. The contractors had seized a favourable opportunity to go into receivership and retire on the proceeds, leaving the work half finished, and because of the ensuing litigation likely to remain so for some time. We found ourselves a comfortable berth under the office windows of the port officials, who happily decided to ignore us.

One of the reasons for rebuilding Milazzo is that the size of merchant ships has increased and the older small harbours no longer have room for them. At Milazzo, an oil refinery loading pier has been built in the bay outside the port, and the super-tankers now stay out there, either at the loading pier or at anchor in the bay. As is the rule in most oil installations, the ships' crews are not allowed to go ashore or to be supplied with victuals along the pier, on which security and safety measures are very strict indeed. All the super-tankers rely for their contact with civilisation on a number of launches which maintain a routine service to and from the old harbour. The administrative office of this service was also near our berth, and as these launches have the same size of diesel engine that we had, Bill went to them for advice on finding a good mechanic.

It turned out that the harbour-master's personal launch had Cummins engines, and we were soon in touch with the Cummins agent for Sicily in Catania. A man vaguely associated with the company in that he had borrowed the Cummins van (so we decided later), turned up one morning, accompanied by a boy. Pietro and Horatio. Arrant rogues, both.

Between them they soon reduced our Cummins engine to a rather dirty kit of parts. It turned out that two cylinders had been full of liquid. One with water and the other with diesel oil, and no satisfactory explanation could be arrived at. The head of the engine was removed to a workshop for skimming and eventually the whole was re-assembled using the gargantuan torque wrench, and then a new water pump was installed. The new water pump cost about the same as a small motor car and it was very difficult to see why. But the engine started. We gave it a three hour run, and though it did not reach its full designed power, we concluded that this was because the ship was moored.

We were very relieved to have the engine working again. Too

relieved to have remembered that DH Lawrence wrote that Sicily:

> '...waits for each and other,
> She waits for all men born,
> What for? To rook them, overcharge them,
> to diddle them and do them down.'

Especially when our two diddlers managed to wheedle a rock music cassette out of us on top of the exorbitant amount they demanded.

Finding the money turned into farce as we trailed round ten different banks to amass the sum, one of them with the untrustworthy sounding name of Banco di Monte dei Paschi di Siena, with Bill's glasses setting off the alarm in almost every one of them.

We stored ship, got a weather forecast, and left. No time, on this visit, to enjoy the other Sicily that we loved, not that of the Mafia and the rippers-off, but an island of golden Greek temples, Roman pavements, and basilicas with brilliant mosaics. We had lost another ten days on the engine repair, the weather report was tolerable, *Siandra* had long left, and was now ahead of us on the journey home.

Unfortunately the tolerability of the weather was less evident when we got off shore. The cats complained, and never liking to admit defeat and go back, we put into Lipari, the biggest of the Aeolian Islands, for shelter, and to await better weather. We were now into May, surely summer could not be far off? Ho Ho Ho.

It was good to be back among small islands again, after Milazzo, where our stay had been stressful to say the least. Islands are so much more intimate than the mainland. To live in an island is to be closer to, and more tolerant of, the forces of nature, more in tune with the realities of life, and in the end, more understanding of people. Life seldom bustles in an island, or only for a short period while the ferry is in, bringing with it the hunger for hurry that characterises mainland communities and temporarily infects the port. When the ferry sails again, the island heaves a collective sigh and relaxes back into a pleasant sloth until the next ferry arrives, please God not too often. Also the shopping is better. An island's shops must be to a certain extent self-sufficient and able to stock a bigger range of goods. So that in a small community you can find within walking distance (best of all *Laurel's* walking distance) the important things that normally are found only in a big town, and then probably in huge stores on the outskirts of bafflingly unsignposted industrial estates.

One problem that constitutes a fly in the island ointment is often the shortage of fresh water, but Lipari had had a wet winter (where had they not?) and they were quite happy to fill our tanks, a happiness that would probably disappear during the tourist season.

We rambled round the little town. Laurel, buying bread in the kind of bakery that has a wood-fired oven behind the shop, had a serious talk with the lady baker, and bought two kilos of a wholemeal flour that she highly recommended for our needs. We also found up a little alley the 'Trattoria del Vicolo', whose English sign read:

> 'Where flavours and pleasant odours bring again
> the memory to the genuineness of once.'

Utterly charmed, we went there that evening to sample the flavours and odours of once. We had a meal of risotto with shellfish, octopus, and *fritto misto*, mixed fried fish. And of course, ice cream and strawberries. On board, we are not great pudding fans, but we love the soft fruit season. We have to admit that from the beginning of April when the strawberry season had arrived in Greece, that is what we had, as often as they were available, which was all the time and everywhere (except in restaurants), and the season followed us north all through France and to England, where it ended in August. For us, it was a bad year for most things but a good year for strawberries.

· 4 ·

RENDEZVOUS WITH DEATH

The stranger is for the wolf. (ARAB PROVERB)

In which we wait for the weather in Sardinia – bad
tidings at the Pirates' Den – the Corsican Mafia – end
of the Mediterranean Sea voyage – we arrive in the
town of Dead-Waters – and our vessel is emastulated

The weather improved a little and we left Lipari for Sardinia, a passage almost as long as the one between Paxos and Italy. It would take 48 hours which we contemplated with some anxiety, but completed in good order, even if the engine, now behaving reasonably well, could only produce three-quarters of its normal power. We entered the small port of La Caletta during the night. We had received a sharply gloomy weather forecast, and were very glad to be there.

La Caletta is halfway down the east coast of Sardinia. Like much of southern Italy, it is very scruffy. Somehow the land that gave us some of the most beautiful painters in the world, wonderful sculptors, superb buildings, poetry, grand opera, Gregorian chant, and the modern system of musical notation, trails into litter, dust, domestic trash, and wirescapes in its more southerly islands. The fact is that even when a civic-minded authority decides to have a clean up, the place still ends up being scruffy. It used to be the same with sailors: one could give the same smart uniforms to two sailors, both the same physical size, and yet one would be the epitome of smartness, while the other could not appear other than a dog's breakfast. Southern Italy has become the municipal dog's breakfast of Europe.

Enormous amounts of European money are being spent in these fringe areas of Europe to stimulate tourism and the results are open to some doubt. Often the agricultural basics are being abandoned for easier tourist money, centuries-old terracing is falling into ruin, and would cost the earth to refurbish if economic conditions changed, and the desert took over. What would these people do if the prosperity of the mainland city folk who come each summer to spend and spend were to be seriously undermined? This is not so unlikely. Already the new catamaran car ferry which had started to operate to La Caletta had been withdrawn and its future was in doubt. The most serious aspect is that the effects of economic depression in the prosperous industrial cities of central Europe are amplified several times when those effects are felt in the fringe areas. Without their basic primitive agriculture to fall back on, these communities could become a heavy millstone round the necks of European industry.

Such is La Caletta with its new yacht harbour only one third full, its moderate shopping rather distant from the harbour, dusty streets and grubby beaches.

After three days waiting for weather we were able to set sail once more. We expected only a short break, but as we approached the Straits of Bonifacio we got the French weather forecast, which held out better prospects than the Italian. We decided we preferred French weather, so we headed across the Straits towards Corsica.

First, though, we had to pass through the Straits of La Maddelena. This narrow (about half a mile wide in places) tortuous channel between the islands of the Maddelena group and Sardinia itself was the scene of one of Nelson's most skilful exploits. Not a battle, but a brilliant and daring bit of seamanship that would give him an edge in a forthcoming engagement. He took the British fleet, which remember, consisted of the huge ungainly ships of the line that were far from being close winded, through these straits against the wind during a moonless dark night. There were no lighthouses, no channel markings; it was feel as you go. One has perhaps to be a seaman in sail fully to appreciate the nautical skills of this little squeaky-voiced, Norfolk-accented, one-eyed, one-armed adulterer who was also a military genius. As we passed in his wake, we poured a libation of Sicilian wine into the sea to his immortal memory.

With the weather continuing reasonable, if not fair, Bill judged it desirable to get out of the treacherous Straits of Bonifacio, so often a place of sudden squalls and unexpected thunderstorms, and round Capo Moro, the south-western tip of Corsica, and this we did, anchoring for a night's rest in the bay close east of the cape.

This bay is not the good anchorage it once was. The authorities have divided it between three users: fish farmers, holiday makers wanting to swim or water-ski, and the yachts. They allow no overlap, and with an alarming lack of nautical sensitivity, have allocated the only area where the depth and type of bottom make a good anchorage for boats to the fish farmers, whose fish are in cages that prevent them diving down anywhere near the bottom, and so are not noticeably conscious, within limits, of the depth of water under them. The fish farms could just as easily be in the deeper parts of the bay, over the rocky bottom which is of no use as an anchorage. The result is that the yachts, who are tourists too, like the campers who have the rest of the shallow area, and who reasonably need that facility for family swimming, have been forced to anchor in the quite unsuitable deep water with a rocky bottom where their anchors do not grip.

This usually provides a lot of fun for spectators, providing their own anchor is holding.

To anchor safely in deep water requires a great length of cable, rather more than a charter yacht would carry. The trouble is that the charts and pilot books of this area still list this as a good anchorage. The consequence is that numbers of charter yachts do anchor there and with insufficient cable too, and it is one of the entertainments of this anchorage to watch them dragging past when the wind gets up. What is not so amusing is that they cannot accept that a prudent seaman will use a lot of cable, and thus require a large swinging circle. When the season has begun, as it manifestly had in Corsica (this was our first encounter with more than one or two yachts since the start of our voyage), we try to make a point of going into these anchorages early in the day; it is the accepted etiquette that boats arriving later have to keep clear of those already settled. We can thus sit there with our solid steel hull and plenty of chain down, and not worry unduly about people swinging into us. It sounds a bit selfish, but the alternative is continually pointing out to unwilling hearers that they are not anchoring safely, and there is a type of modern yachtsman who strongly resents advice, however tactfully put.

For much the same reason, that is to arrive early, we set off the next morning before breakfast for a quick hop up the west coast of Corsica to Girolata, perhaps our favourite Corsican anchorage.

We have used it often and had become friends with the eccentric Parisien who had a beach-bar cum restaurant right on the shore. He and his staff were out and out show-biz, 'out' being the correct word. Jacky liked to dress as closely as he could to Corto Maltese, a popular adult comic strip hero, who is a tall handsome English Naval Officer of the early 1900s. Jacky managed pretty well, down to the single earring and cheesecutter Naval cap, but was about a foot too short. He was living in a dream; he was very hospitable, and even though we realized that he not only loved *Hosanna* but fancied the Captain as well, he was a very good host. He had provided at his primitive log-cabin establishment 'Le Repère des Pirates' all the necessities that a yachtsman, while seeking to enjoy unsophistication, appreciates having access to, like bread, wine, and the weather forecast. We had spent a memorable evening dining on our last visit, waited on by Denis (who had two earrings, and had learnt the art of putting a plate down without jingling six inches of assorted silver bangles), followed by so much of Jacky's cognac, on the house, that we couldn't remember rowing back to the boat.

Even in a hurry, we could not have failed to call on Jacky.

Girolata is a small anchorage, but it is shallow and sheltered, and a good number of boats can lie there in safety. So we were surprised to find the bay empty; and our delight at being able to choose just the right spot for our big anchor was tempered by dismay to see through the binoculars that 'Le Repère des Pirates' was closed. For the afternoon perhaps, we thought, it being not yet full season. Or perhaps they are not yet open at all; it looked very firmly shuttered.

About six we rowed ashore to take our rubbish for the bin, which Bill had to chase up the track where it was being towed away by a tractor. We intended to have a drink and see about some supper. We became a bit more worried now about our old friends; the tractor driver had seemed

unwilling to give us any news. We ordered a drink at the neighbouring bar, La Cabane du Berger (the Shepherd's Hut). We were hospitably received by a youngish looking Shepherd and his pretty wife, but it was not quite the same as The

Pirates' Lair. Where was Jacky Martin? Still in Paris? we asked.

There was an awkward silence, which seemed to last a very long time. 'You have not then heard?' said the Shepherd. 'He was assassinated. A boat came by night. Jacky and his *copain* were both murdered by shotgun. I will give you a flask of my own wine, you will drink to the memory.' We sat down, shaken and silent, and drank.

It took time to get even some sort of story from various sources. Two men wearing masks had disembarked and shot Jacky and Denis at point blank range with a sawn-off shotgun. There was no robbery. The murderers left by fast boat. No one called the police. Nobody saw anything. Nobody was ever charged. It seemed that it had happened very shortly after our last visit, when Jacky had written in our visitor's book: 'Delicately yours, *avec toutes nos amitiés pour l'eternité*' ...our kind regards for eternity. Eternity had come for Jacky unexpectedly and with violence.

With no concrete evidence, only a feeling that we got by putting together the atmosphere and the body language of those who turned away as they shrugged off our questions, we formed our own loose conclusion.

We were not very familiar with the tourist's Corsica. The glossy brochures of the Isle of Beauty showed the sunseeker something similar to Porto Cervo in Sardinia, where we had once wandered ashore bemused by the sanitised artificial glitter of it; Corsica too, the brochures seemed to say, was a millionaire's paradise of lovely beaches, purpose built resorts, and a carefully censored glimpse of romantic but sleazy old streets in Calvi or Olbia. Away from enclaves where all seems expected and familiar, the real wild country is still there and is very different. The mountains are savage and grow a people to match. Girolata, a narrow cleft in a mountainous coast, has only recently been approachable by road. We imagined the feelings of the local people, faced with aliens from Paris, opening a restaurant on their beach, and being not only successful but gay. Our host at the Shepherd's Hut was Corsican, born nearby, and spoke French like us: as a foreign language. To his wife he spoke Corsican. It was the Feast of

Ascension and our host gave Laurel a tiny glass pot, containing a succulent which flowers in those mountains only at Ascensiontide. The plant lasted a long time after the flowers had gone, and Laurel often wondered as she looked at it if the smiling eyes of the giver had looked through a mask, and if his hands had held a shotgun.

We passed a quiet night at Girolata, and left the next morning. It was set fair, not a breath of wind, and with a forecast of increasing easterlies we pressed on towards France, taking advantage of the good conditions to do another long hop.

At half past nine in the evening we raised the Cap Camaret lighthouse on the Ile de Levant, and in the small hours we wound our way through the tricky but familiar passage between the islands that leads to the Baie des Langoustiers, where, at four thirty in the morning, with silent apologies to the sleeping yachts clustered there, we let the anchor go with a rattle and pitched into bed for a few hours sleep.

The following day was taken up by fuelling and storing in Porquerolles, and it was not till evening that we set sail again, this time bound for the mainland of France. We found the Port St Louis entrance to the river Rhône had been closed for repair, so had another forty miles to go to reach Le-Grau-du-Roi at the western end of the Camargue. The easterlies had begun and the sea became choppy. The night was uncomfortable, the lighthouse at Faraman seemed to take a long while to pass. The day dawned grey and misty, and porridge made a welcome breakfast, even though this was mid May; and it was with some relief that we said goodbye to the sea for a while as we glided into harbour and made fast to the fishquay at Le-Grau-du-Roi. The sea part of the voyage was over until we reached the English Channel.

Twenty months previously we had left Le-Grau-du-Roi eastbound and we had reached Turkey before returning. One of the fishermen in the boat behind us hailed us as old friends as indeed we were: Serge, who had been a waiter but was now much happier fishing, bronzed and longhaired instead of the cropped and tidy *garçon* who had once served us our Sunday drinks at L'Express. The boats were coming in to shelter, there was a gale warning, he said, and we felt even happier to be safely in ourselves. He gave us our first accolade when we told him where we had come from. 'Greece! Ai-yai-yai! That's a *beau voyage!*'

The bridges would not be opening again till six that evening, so we could spend an enjoyable day. It was not too late for a second breakfast of fresh croissants. The cats stopped scolding us for a bad night at sea, demanded food, washed, and swaggered ashore to pull rank over the local moggies. In so doing they fortunately missed an egret who settled on our forerail, preening its snowy feathers, as if to welcome us back; surely an omen of good fortune.

It seemed not. We have made the passage through the two bridges at Grau many times, and most of them have been full of unwanted incident, to the point where sphincters now tighten on the approach.

This time there was no cross wind, thank goodness. The bridgemaster seemed in a good temper for once; we suspected him of delaying the opening on occasions, just for the fun of getting us into difficulties, as the second bridge is very narrow and on a bend, and impeded by the town pontoons. He had been known to refuse to open at all if he was really out of temper. We saw the bridge begin to lift, and began to get into place, which necessitated turning sharp right close after the end pontoon and lining up all our 86 feet to pass through the bridge, and very little space to do it in.

You can imagine our dismay when, as the bridge opened, a medium sized Swedish yacht appeared on the other side and dashed immoderately through the opening straight at our bows. We were almost stopped at this point, making perhaps half a knot through the water, and almost unable to turn. But that was not all! Boats in channels are required to keep to the right: we had positioned ourselves to the right of the channel, and watched with horror as the Swede swung sharply over to his left and tried to land somebody on the last pontoon, ravaging our line-up strategy. Only our going emergency full astern could have saved him from being crushed, and this caused some delay as we had to re-establish our position. We were both mortally afraid that the bridge would close before we got through, knowing the *pontier's* penchant for playing games. It is difficult manoeuvring large craft close to small ones dashing about like terriers, and the rules make special provision for such cases, rules unknown to the Swede, it seemed. Bill's comment to the Skipper as we passed on our way to the bridge was: 'You are a very silly man,' which Laurel found astonishingly mild. Perhaps we should add that such antics are rare from Swedes, who are normally competent boat handlers.

We found a mooring an hour later at the yacht station under the massive old walls of the little city of Aigues-Mortes.

We have described the Camargue and the two towns to its west in some detail in a previous book*, but a little recapitulation is necessary here, to explain why we again succumbed to lotus-eating. The ramparts surrounding Aigues-Mortes are probably the best example of a mediaeval curtain wall anywhere, being largely unrestored yet in good condition. The town was built by Louis IX, Saint Louis, as a home base for his crusades, on the last of which he died of plague in Tunis. His crusades were completely unsuccessful, but his death while so engaged, helped by an unblemished record of justice and integrity, ensured his beatification. Richard the First, who eighty years earlier had been a far more successful Crusader seeing that he took Acre and then went on almost to Jerusalem where he succeeded in bringing Saladin to a truce that gave Christians access to the Holy Sepulchre, had to be content with the sobriquet, Lionheart. His CV for sainthood obviously left a good deal to be desired.

During our previous stay in this beautiful town we had enjoyed many adventures and made many friends. We noticed some absences, but were welcomed by Serge II, the proprietor of the *Pescalune*, a Dutch barge like our own, but converted to take holiday makers round the waters of the Petite Camargue to see the white horses, flamingoes, the salt flats, the black bulls and the egrets, a tour which gave its passengers excellent value. Business for all had increased since our last visit, the waterway was crowded.

* *A Spell in Wild France*

There was just enough room for us in the yacht harbour, so we paid for one day and spent it lowering the masts, which we do by ourselves. An alongside berth in a popular resort is not the best place to do this, as lowering three masts, two of them weighing 300 kilos each, and their spars, is heavy work, requiring intense concentration if we are not to damage the boat, the gear, or ourselves. It is not possible to explain to interested but unknowledgable passers-by that a moment's distraction could lead to a fatal accident.

Now is the moment to apologise to all the bewildered tourists who have watched us do this and wanted answers to their questions, for our terse and sometimes non-existent replies. Please come back when we've finished, and the masts are safely down, and we'll talk all you want.

In the meantime the winch drum is under Laurel's charge, and must be closely watched to avoid a riding (that is a jamming) turn of the rope which is lowering the mast. A watch must be kept for wash from boats going too fast, and operations suspended until the water settles, as a half-lowered mast with a sway on can be very difficult to deal with. The lowering manoeuvre is slow and deliberate, with many stops to ensure nothing is caught up or binding or getting damaged. You can understand that with the mainmast halfway down, and a speedboat churning up the water and causing it to sway, our heart sinks when a voice calls from quayside: 'I say … can I ask you something!'

We got the mainmast down in the morning, the foremast in the afternoon. We then had a thorough wash down and filled the water tanks, before lowering the mizzen mast. Then, being now in canal mode, we passed under the road bridge and through the rail bridge into the Bassin d'Evolution at the gates of Aigues-Mortes. As there was nowhere to berth, Serge II invited us to lie alongside *Pescalune* for a couple of nights, knowing that we would happily move when necessary so he could get in and out with his tourists. We settled down to spend a day or two seeing friends, catching up on the news, and relaxing, before we began the long canal journey to Calais and England.

· 5 ·

WRONG WAY UP THE RHÔNE

The hardest biscuit goes to the seaman with fewest teeth. (GREEK PROVERB)

In which we lament the passing of the van rouge – the weather turns again – we beware of Dracs and Lerts and encounter dangerous current

Since we had had a tough day lowering the masts and washing down, we treated ourselves to a meal ashore.

This is something to be embarked on with caution in a holiday resort where there are many restaurants, but a dearth of good chefs. All the same, sitting out on a May evening under the plane trees in the square is in itself such a delight that we allowed ourselves to be ripped off in return for the atmosphere. The next evening we returned to our old haunt, L'Escale, only 50 yards away from the boat, outside the ramparts, where we were welcomed back and made at home. The cuisine at L'Escale is bourgeoise rather than haute, but one can eat there very inexpensively as do the local working people and a few discerning tourists. The controversial municipal toilets occupying part of the outlook over the *Bassin*, the only underground toilets to be built above ground as we once described them*, were now hardly less evident under some desperate municipal plantings of berberis. The Tree of Liberty planted at the toilet door to mark the Bicentennaire was struggling, but alive. There was no commemorative plaque yet: the mayor was probably waiting to see if the tree would thrive.

We took on fuel, did some shopping, entertained dozens of visitors, picked up our mail and prepared to depart.

---

* See *A Spell in Wild France.*

47

It was time to move on, because the aim was England; we were still a long way south and though rushing at any time was strongly against our philosophy, we were already late.

One kilometre up the canal our philosophy was again at complete loggerheads with our declared intentions and won us a couple of hours alongside the barge *L'Escaut*, in which live our friends Daniel and Francine, with whom we had shared many adventures*. We were treated, deliciously, to more of the local gossip.

Bernard, who lived in the barge *Massabielle* with an enormous family, was in gaol. We were sorry to hear this, as he had often helped us with mechanical problems in the past. It has to be pointed out that the community of barge dwellers, of which we are examples, consists not only of respectable citizens, some titled, some of humble origin and means, but a rich tapestry of others whose imaginative activities are of dubious legality. Such is Bernard, whose barge was fitted out as if for a crusader's siege, with enough food for months, with cages of rabbits and chickens, dried fruit and vegetables, strings of onions and garlic, the whole guarded by perpetually chained and snarling dogs. He allowed no one other than other barge people near his boat, officials and police were excluded, and he met all strangers with a shotgun at the ready.

We were not wholly surprised to find that he was in gaol, expecting to hear that he had at last shot someone, or carved his initials on them with an axe (he was noted for living on a short fuse), but that was not the cause. His crime was not a violent one and it should have come as no surprise to us.

When we had first met Bernard years ago and had been shown the astonishing contents of his barge, he had told us that his wife was the breadwinner of the family. 'I put her out to work,' he grinned. Himself, he did some gardening to stock his larders, messed about with old cars, did engineering jobs for friends (he was a trained artificer) and when the mood took him, shot at people.

It was a while before we realised that Paulette gained the family living from the oldest profession. Her place of work

* See *A Spell in Wild France.*

48

was a main road lay-by a few kilometres from Aigues-Mortes on which she would park her specially fitted Ford Transit camionette, appropriately painted red. We had passed it several times before we recognised it as the same van that parked among the bangers alongside *Massabielle*. We put two and two together and guessed at a nice little earner, which we had christened 'Le Van Rouge'. We had discovered that a Van Rouge is not at all uncommon in the lay-byes of France, seemingly tolerated by officialdom as doing little harm while offering an essential service along with the Chippie and the ice cream van. Why, therefore, had Bernard and his wife been singled out for the authorities' malice?

They had long been after Bernard, mainly because he delighted in provoking them, but nothing of any seriousness could be made to stick, possibly for lack of prosecution witnesses. This time the authorities succeeded with a charge of *proxenitisme*, which is the French name for living off immoral earnings. We once recalled an old Suffolk boy who had reported in the bar of the General Wolfe Inn that so-and-so had been charged with living off immoral Ernies. In this case it was immoral Bernies. Bernard had got three months and the Van Rouge had turned to vinegar.

We were sorry to miss Bernard, who is, like most barge dwellers, an interesting character and good company, a person from whom one can learn many and surprising things. It should also be pointed out that in the wild places of France (such as here in the Camargue), it does no harm to be known as the friend of one who settles arguments, not by reasoning, but by decisive and unilateral means. If shotguns are to be part of the scenery, make sure they are on your side. After a refreshing couple of hours, meeting old friends and new babies, all fatherless, we left northbound.

This was the start of the long plug up the rivers and canals the whole length of France, 1400 odd kilometres to Calais. When we later discovered that this day, 22 May, was under the tutelage of one of the bargees' favourite saints, Ste Rita, the saint of the impossible, we felt that it was entirely appropriate.

We soon met our first check, at the first of the 208 locks on our route: the Ecluse de St Gilles, a flood control lock that lets the canal out onto the broad river (contrarily called Le Petit Rhône), which in turn leads out to the sea. (Not for yachts, though, as there is a two metre high cable across it at one point, and a very shallow harbour bar at the entrance.)

In the weeks we had spent travelling from Greece, a series of depressions had swept across the middle of France depositing unusually heavy rainfall in the mountains, in which the winter's snow was already melting. By now all this water had reached the Rhône, the water level was above normal, the flood gates on the Rhône side were closed. We were met with the famous French cry: '*Ils ne passeront pas*' (They shall not pass). This is an example of the way in which a simple saying by a comparative unknown becomes heavily edited and then transformed into a national monument, finally being attributed to a more famous person. What General Nivelle wrote in his daily orders at Verdun in 1916 was:

'*Vous ne les laisserez pas passer*' (You shall not let them pass), a phrase far too full of sibilants ever to become truly historic. It is not nearly as dramatic as the amended quotation, and General Nivelle was not nearly as well known a figure as Marshal Pétain, to whom the saying is usually mis-attributed. Marshal Pétain went on to become notorious for enthusiastically encouraging the Germans to pass wherever they liked, so in our view disqualifying himself for ever as the author of a good quotation.

In the meantime we could not pass.

A consultation with the lock-keeper reassured us that the level was dropping rapidly, and if we would patient ourselves we would undoubtedly be rewarded; a matter of only an hour or two.

We did some chores while waiting, and had a tidy up, and remembered to count the cats before we left.

When we did pass the lock, we found that the current was running strongly and though we used all the power our dicey engine could give, we were only just able to make headway against the swollen river. It was probably unwise to try to buck nature in this way; normally we would have waited, but our carefully designed timetable was getting more and more behind, so we plugged on into the Rhône itself. Normally Laurel would have shared the driving, but to coax the maximum effort from a failing engine under difficult circumstances, the expertise of a master was required. The worst trouble occurred in the confines of the old city of Beaucaire. Here, where the river thundered down the narrows under two bridges, we stared aghast as we saw the water racing past the abutments, forming a bow wave against the pillars like a tanker at speed, with the water level a foot higher on the upstream side, like a huge step in the water. We had plenty of

Laurel.

time to watch it, fascinated, as we inched painfully past. Unable now to use the slacker water at the river's edge, we had no choice but to stem the stream at its strongest, right in the centre, in order to pass under the arches. We could almost hear the mocking laughter of the Drac, the evil genie of the Rhône who haunts the waters at Beaucaire, and the snickering of his crew of Nerks, Bluques, Dahuts and other gobbledegook folklorical beings who inhabit the more spectacular reaches of the Rhône, waiting to drag poor sailors under. Small wonder the Saints of the bargees are called upon continuously for aid, as if they were a celestial Automobile Club.

The maximum adverse current we measured here against the kilometre posts was 10 kilometres per hour, but it must have been stronger under the bridges at Beaucaire.

It seemed hours before we were sufficiently clear of the narrows to slink back to the marginally less rampageous waters away from midstream. We continued on till dusk, passing through the lock at Vallabrègues.

Here, very tired, we moored for the night to the *ducs d'Albe*, or dolphins: heavy piles driven into the bed of the river for ships to make fast to. These are about 33 metres apart, a convenient length for a standard 38 m *péniche* (barge) but far enough apart to cause us some minor inconvenience. One hangs between the two like shirt on a washing line. There are no facilities at all for smaller pleasure craft to moor at these locks. One compensation, if we could not get ashore, nor could the cats, so they were given the freedom to race round the deck all night.

We were away next morning into a beautiful day. We passed up the delights of Avignon, one of our favourite cities, because to enjoy a place like this requires at the least a few days to attune oneself, and we had to resist the temptation. At Aramon we experienced the strongest current we had so far measured, 12 km per hour.

The weather was so much in contrast to the previous time we had passed this way that we deliberately moored for lunch alongside the little quay at Rochemaure, where on a previous visit during a mistral we had been so dangerously uncomfortable*. The pebbles which had then been glazed with ice were now hidden under a carpet of wild flowers, much appreciated by the cats who were allowed briefly ashore under surveillance.

Our previous long day's travel had left us both weary, and coming across a good mooring at St Etienne-des-Sorts at four in the afternoon, we stopped early and moored for the night alongside a large floating crane. We had no choice of position, because the crane had installed itself in dead centre of the quay, so as to leave inadequate room and bollards at either end. We have often observed that the first to arrive has an irresistible tendency to occupy the exact middle of the available quay. It is necessary to have very strict self-discipline to make fast to the end of an otherwise empty quay thus leaving a later

---

* See *Watersteps Through France*

arrival with room to berth, and this form of self-discipline is characteristic of a good seaman.

This early stop enabled us to enjoy a little walk round the village, during which we found a restaurant some 600 metres to the north, with an appetising menu, but firmly closed. It was a Monday. France fasts on a Monday, everyone knows that. Chefs are all sleeping off a busy Sunday. Still we did not eat badly on board; Laurel had bought some fresh produce at a stall in the village, and as we had missed our Sunday roast on yesterday's long haul, we had it now: roast duck, which she garnished with slices of orange marinaded in oriental spices, brilliant in Bill's opinion, and fresh green peas, the kind with pods that have to be shucked. We shared a bottle of good Minervois, a much under-rated Bordeaux-style wine. For dessert we had fresh cherries, and strawberries again. We live well in our boat; being afloat does not necessarily deprive one of luxuries. As dusk fell, the cats found the crane a wonderful workout gymnasium. While we were watching them, we noticed a small yacht southbound and waved him alongside. He overshot by only a few yards, but took quarter of an hour stemming the current back to us. There were no other moorings for a long way, we told him. So *Emma of Chatham* spent the night alongside us, and we enjoyed the usual sort of boaty mardle that is so much a part of the cruising life.

Next morning it was grey and raining and *Emma* left early. Laurel visited the market while Bill mopped up the results of a leaky connection on the fuel oil return pipe which had left us with a few pints of diesel oil in our bilges. We normally reckon to keep our bilges pristine and clean them with a hoover, so it was a priority job to tighten the joint, and then empty and clean the bilge with detergent. Once upon a time we would have followed the general practice of seamen (and others, too) everywhere and discharged the mess overboard into God's great gash bin, which is what one had heard it called. In those days the amount of oil used at sea was very small, and it probably did little total harm, but we have accepted that with so many craft using so much oil, we must take care. The oil was soaked up into kitchen paper and burned in our stove.

The following day our experience of conditions began to show that the current was often strongest just below a lock, and usually weaker just above, for what reason we cannot say as the river was much the same width throughout and the same volume of water was passing.

During this day we reached the point we had most dreaded: the Defilé de Donzère, where the torrent rushes through a narrow gorge three kilometres long. Most of these dread passages are under the tutelage of some *marinier's* Saint, usually St Nicholas, or St Roch. Here the oversight of a full Archangel is required, St Michael himself, and we tossed a plea in his beneficent direction and hoped for mercy. Though bridled by extensive hydro-electric schemes, the current was the strongest yet, a minimum of 12 km per hour, and we had to creep up the edges of the channel within a boathook's length of the bank to try to avoid the worst of the current, hoping all the time that piles of debris had not been dumped near the banks of the swollen river for us to run aground on. The French seem to be of two extremes in this respect: there are those who very carefully sort their rubbish into bags of different types and search out the specially provided colour coded bins for paper, green bottles, white bottles, metal, foodstuffs, plastics, and so on. Others, less green, merely throw everything into the nearest canal or river. To be fair, the former type are gaining, but one *irresponsable* can undo all the efforts of a dozen good citizens, and we reflected that just one discarded washing machine or refrigerator left in the comparative shallows where we were trying to navigate would do us more harm that all the Dracs, Lerts and Dahuts of the mythical past.

It also came to us as we clawed our way upstream, in a state only just below that of panic, that in spite of its 'taming', the Rhône can still be a terrifying river. No wonder the rivermen of times gone by feared it and peopled it with supernatural beings. For one thing, it seems to be one of the few masculine rivers in France. The words for a river vary between *le fleuve*, masculine and signifying a river that flows to the sea, and *la rivière*, feminine, signifying a tributary. (Feminists, please be quiet for a minute.) However, the big river names themselves carry a gender that does not conform as a rule to the descriptive noun. Thus La Seine, La Gironde, La Loire are masculine fleuves in spite of their feminine names. Le Rhône however is thoroughly masculine right to the last drop, perhaps because it is masculine by nature? Rough, unreliable, difficult to tame, and dangerous? Like the bull which is one of its Provençal names.

We would often like to put in a plea that, if the French really want to see themselves accepted as the great arbiters of logical thought and their language a world language, they could help their cause by removing some of its remarkable inconsistencies. There are, we suggest, two reasons why they do not. One is tradition. To the French there are some things connected with *La Patrimoine* that are immutable. *Ils ne changeront pas*. Logic, convenience, ridicule even, nothing can change them. The other reason, which is partly contained in the first, is poetry.

Two features of poetry that are dear to English poets generally are rhyming and alliteration. French poetry is not very strong on alliteration; it is an Anglo Saxon concept, foreign to them. The French poets use rhyme of course, but they also use the gender of words to express poetical nuances and symbolism. It is a poetic weapon which is lost to us, or perhaps we have never had. It is interesting that we have never come across references to this convention in works on Latin or Greek poetry. The Romans and Greeks had their genders: was it a feature with them, and if so, do French readers of classical poetry get more from it than we do? We think we should be told.

· 6 ·

COPING ON OUR RHÔNE

In which the currents run counter – we are boarded by
forty natives – our monster suffers a mortal blow – at
Lyon we miss a Pardon and face a difficult task

Once through the gorge at Donzère and the lock at Bollène, huge as a concrete cathedral, the way was easier, and after the next lock the run to Montelimar, where the nougat comes from, was not eventful. It began to rain and it was difficult to find a mooring. We eventually made fast to an enormous and otherwise empty quay that was over ten metres high, constructed of huge baulks of timber, some of it in a very poor state. We made fast near the only steps let into the quay, and Bill went up to fasten extra ropes to the bollards at the very top, he having decided that with the possibility of flood water, the small brackets which were all that existed at the lower level were not strong enough to hold us under all circumstances. He's like that, is Bill. Laurel took one look at the rotten timbers and shut the cats in. As it was by now pouring with rain, they did not object.

At the top, in the centre of a vast expanse of concrete was a coach, and watching but not helping us, was the driver who asked if we had seen a boatload of children on the way.

'That must be the *Calabrun*,' replied Bill. 'We passed her at a landing stage further down the river.'

'That's right. She was due here at 1830.'

'Well the river is running very strongly. She will be late.'

It was already after eight. The coach driver looked at his watch and sighed. Bill walked gingerly down the awkward steps, slippery with chemicals that had been spilled from

56

barges loading or unloading cargoes, and which had obviously never been cleaned up. They can't be planning to use these steps, he thought.

They were, because there were no others. At about half past eight the *Calabrun* arrived. We offered to lay off to let the children disembark, but the skipper agreed with us that it would be easier to get the forty children, all aged under eight, onto our deck where there were safety guard rails, before trying to get them onto the slippery platform at the bottom of the quay's stairs, which had no hand rail.

He berthed in the sluicingly strong stream (alliteration again!), and we observed some very professional schoolteachers in action. They disposed themselves carefully at the danger points, and one stayed on board the *Calabrun* to check each child before handing it over to our boat. Each child was made to put his satchel over the left shoulder so that it would be easier to lift the children bodily, always from the same side, and always with the teacher twisting the same way. With such a load of little monsters it could easily have disintegrated into chaos, but it all went superbly smoothly. There were the two crew of *Calabrun*, three teachers, and ourselves stationed at various points up the very unsafe steps passing the children from hand to hand. The children were tired, but obedient.

Would this have been similar in Britain? Perhaps. Dedicated and skilful teachers are found in all communities. Would our bureaucrats have permitted disembarkation steps used by passenger boats to have deteriorated so? In theory no, but we expect that in theory the French are the same. Nevertheless, whatever nationality, we take our hats off to those three teachers who coped with an unexpected problem in an exemplary fashion.

Wednesday the 25th saw us crawling northward once more, with the current stronger still. Under the great cooling towers of the Nuclear Energy Centre at Cruas, sprouting cloud like prize cauliflowers, we had again to plug our way into a current which at the edges of the stream (where it was perhaps only 50% of its midstream strength) was running at 13 kilometres per hour. We kept close to the banks whenever possible and coaxed our lame duck to keep swimming.

We arrived at Logis Neuf lock after a three kilometre struggle with the current at its worst, cutting our speed to four kilometres an hour, about two knots. At this point it seemed a very long way to England. The cheery lock-keeper told us that the water was running at 2500 cubic metres a second, only 300 more, he said happily, and all pleasure navigation would be stopped. This was not good news. We were doing our Rhône thing slowly enough as it was, without Authority stepping in and stopping the Navigation for several days.

Lunchtime at La Voulte was a sandwich snatched without stopping; here, where the town is so picturesquely dominated by church and belltower, demanding to be photographed, is another place justly dreaded by the *mariniers* of old, who would undoubtedly have called upon one or more of the saints in charge of *passages difficiles*. There were many of these Saints, as it was a twenty-four hour a day job to protect *mariniers* engaged on dangerous journeys. One imagines them drawing up a roster to make sure that some Saint or other was on duty at any given time. Here we were faced with the prospect of going towards midstream to pass under a restricted bridge, where the current was at its strongest. Whichever saint was on duty that day did his stuff and we arrived safely at Tournon, though mooring there was not easy.

There is a little backwater to the north of the main quay, which has moorings out of the very strong current, so much out of it that entry to the backwater was difficult: at one point the current was flowing at about 10 km/hr across the entry and a few yards further on it was eddying in the opposite direction, making manoeuvring a longish boat into a narrow space that was almost full of other craft a bit of a nightmare. We succeeded without hitting anybody. These problems serve to keep the grey matter churning, which is why boats are very good for older people. A crisis a day keeps senility at bay, we told ourselves, full of optimism, and took time to admire our situation.

Above us beetled the machicolations of an ancient tower, set among the purlieus of the 16th century castle that forms the heart of Tournon. Here in these harsh and uncompromising walls the Dauphin François died at the age of 19, and the poet

Ronsard, there as page to the Court, wrote that the Rhône wept for him. The stones are today softened by green and gardened terraces. The quay is shady and treelined, as they are apt to be in these lovely towns of Provence and the Rhône Valley, this one a little less lovely for being exhaustively dug up in a frantic effort to improve something boringly municipal: the drains perhaps. The French never do this by halves; tons of earth are moved, huge holes enthusiastically dug, the traffic rerouted round the suburbs, and those poor tourists like us who want to get from their boat to the quayside restaurant 'La Chaumière' that beckons with a desperate handwritten notice saying OUVERT, will have to get their fellwalking gear on and mountaineer over scree and stone and asphalt precipice to its very doorstep. It had once had a view of the river, now blocked by a middle school built, hideously rectangular, at the river's edge. This was all the more insensitive as the town justly prides itself on another riverside building, a beautiful 16th century one, in which the ancient Lycée was housed.

We found the restaurant had been deleted from the *Guide Michelin*, because it had changed hands. As the new owner was the former *chef de cuisine*, we did not allow this to worry us, and happily noshed into *quenelles de brochet*, those light melt-in-the-mouth pike dumplings, which are to English dumplings as meringue is to yorkshire pudding. Nothing wrong with either; but dumplings and yorkshire pudding seldom come with crayfish sauce. Bill had crisp-skinned *magret de canard,* while Laurel had a favourite light dish, *darne de saumon* with sorrel, which one can cook at home now that freeze-dried sorrel is available. The chocolate mousse was home made, and one cannot ask for more, when so many of them are packet-born: it must be a question of price, as it takes no longer to make the real thing. It could also be a matter of hygiene, as there would be no danger of salmonella, one supposes, from a packet containing powdered egg.

After the short walk back to the boat we had a good night's sleep.

The river flow had increased the next day to the critical 2800 tonnes (the equivalent of cubic metres) per second. We phoned the lock. No, pleasure navigation had not yet been *formally* suspended, but was, one might say *fortement déconseillé*. We agreed to be strongly discouraged. We stayed where we were and went shopping in the first of many thunderstorms.

The next day was fine, but the current still ran hard. When we had finished our chores, we explored again and found in the main street a cheese shop of outstanding excellence and a proprietor whose knowledge was impressive. We bought cheese, some to keep and some to eat fresh: the locally made *fromage frais de brebis*, or cottage cheese made with sheep's milk in the valley of the Ardèche, a favourite of Bill's and something we hunt for in local markets, not always successfully. It was superb.

Across the river we could see sloped in the sunshine the vineyards of Tain l'Hermitage, Tournon's cross-river companion. Here grow some of the best of the Côte du Rhône wines, both white and red. We took the footbridge and went to look at them.

The following day when the flow of water lessened and it was possible to move on at last, we set out northward again.

We had not gone far when the note of the Cummins changed and the engine began to run very roughly. Laurel drove the boat while Bill changed the fuel filters and that seemed to help for most of the day's run, but then in the evening at Vaugris Lock the engine came to a halt while idling. We had to quit the lock immediately on the Perkins only and limped very slowly the remaining 4H km to Vienne where we berthed at the only convenient quay under a sign that said 'Reserved, under dire penalty for misuse, for the pleasure boat *Elle et Lui* by order of the Prefecture'. It was by now very late and raining. Pleasure, they call it.

Half an hour later the pleasure boat *Elle et Lui* arrived, and we explained our problem and apologised profusely. They smiled away our apologies; we had left them room enough to discharge their half-dozen passengers and they would be leaving straightaway. Another good reason for berthing at the end of an empty quay!

Pleased and grateful, we stayed put. The quay was extremely noisy being alongside a main road with traffic lights, but we closed down, shut the cats in for the night and slept very well after an extremely late but splendid dinner of home cooked Osso Buco. Laurel had been able to stock up with Arborio rice as we passed Sicily, which makes all the difference to the Risotto Milanese that goes with this dish.

On Sunday 29 May we pressed on again after Bill had worked for a couple of hours on the Cummins and had got it going, albeit roughly and only at 1000 revs per minute. 'Who is in charge of this stretch? The Archangel Michael seems to have lost interest,' grumbled Laurel.

So, alas, had all the other saints. The engine ran for about ninety minutes before its revs started to drop down and down, with both of us unconsciously assisting it with grunts and gestures of encouragement, until at last, in mid afternoon, it failed completely. This time, no kiss of life in the form of filter cleaning revived it.

There was a long silence, as the implications of this came home. It looked as if our journey had ended and we were still more than a thousand kilometres short of Calais. Our expensive repair in Sicily had lasted twenty four days. We switched on the little Perkins and went on, very slowly.

We were within a few kilometres of Lyon, which is the point at which the Rhône turns east towards its source in the Swiss Alps. Traffic for Calais continues north on the Saône, which has not quite the same deadly reputation as the Rhône, though it can sometimes flow quite fast. Could we beat the last few kilometres and get to Lyon and the Saône?

Laurel's *Book of Useful Saints for Mariners* was at first no help at all. There were Saints for Tempests, for Drownings, for Maladies and Epidemics (mostly very specific) and the already cited Saints for Bridges and Difficult Passages, but none for Mechanical Breakdown. In trouble, all sailors are believers, and need something to shriek to. But to whom? Not St Roch, for Dog Bites, or Ste Geneviève who chases away Serpents, and we were certainly not quite ready for Ste Marguerite-Marie Alacoque, whom sailors invoke for a good death. Ste Rita, for Desperate Causes, began to occupy the background of our minds, the front, we are sorry to say, being taken up with the mundane practicalities of urging on a crippled boat.

61

Perhaps it wasn't St Michael's day off after all, we thought. It seemed as if we were past the worst of the current, but we only just made it across the mouth of a faster flowing confluence below the Pierre Bénite lock which we finally reached in the late afternoon. After that, it became a bit easier and we motored slowly into the mouth of the river Saône at Lyon.

This is where all the Saints were, we discovered. They had gone to a party. As we turned the bend into the Saône we saw the streaming banners and flags, bright against the blackhulled barges who flew them, and the Chapel barge in their midst. It was the day of the *pardon*, a religious festival for the

commercial barges, though anyone on the river is welcome.
There were so many boats that they stretched almost across
the river and we had difficulty passing. Flags were flying everywhere and there was much joy. They waved to us to join them,
but we were full of anxiety, desperately tired and now it was
evening the festival was nearly over. A barge moved to let us
past, and further on at the Quai Maréchal Joffre we found all
the berths empty. We moored up at the far end, away from the
Bourse, or Bureau d'Affrètement where the barge cargoes are
allocated, and settled in.

The barges reberthed close by shortly after our arrival,
dispersing from their festival. The bargefolk are mostly very
religious, and though many bargees especially those from the
north and east, are Protestant, it is generally the Roman
Catholics who make a joyous pageant of their religion. These

pardons or blessings, take place annually in most of the barge centres, and we, as barge dwellers, knew we would have been welcome. Apart from *Hosanna* being badly in need of the benison, it would have been a great party. We chatted to a young Dutch bargee who had attended. The priest had personally cooked a wonderful Couscous at midday, he said. Our mouths watered, and Laurel, inspired, set to building a chicken curry for supper.

When the commercial barges berth at Lyon, and in other places where the public walk on the quay in numbers, they berth at an angle with their bows pinched in to the quay and their sterns held out a few metres away from the edge. There is no nautical reason for this, it is a question of privacy; their quarters are in the stern and they do not like curious passers-by peering into their polished brass portholes. They are beginning to get wary now that they are becoming rarer on the scene, and too many passers-by have camcorders.

There are two ways of tackling a Monday morning. One is to pull the covers over your head and declare an extra Sunday. The other is to regard it as the start of a new week, here and now, and hope that it will be better than the last. If our philosophy of never hurrying was at present deactivated, at least we had held to another of our tenets: always break down, or be delayed, in good surroundings. This had been fulfilled at Tournon, and now, if this was journey's end, we were again in clover. Only about a square metre of it, but there we were.

The Quai Maréchal Joffre is a quiet spot in the centre of Lyon, down below the noise and bustle of street level. It has stone setts, benches, ornamental planting, huge trees and almost no vehicular traffic. The cats loved it. At lunchbreak it is where the Lyonnais bring their partners for a little nookie, and is therefore a good berth for voyeurs. There was excellent shopping, entertainment and food within reasonable distance. There was also a Cummins Head Office.

We needed a break to do some considering. Bill has done much research into the subject of Canal Effect. It was for a time his specialist subject, and was now extremely relevant, being the study of how ships motor, steer and manoeuvre in shallow water, which is not at all the same as in deeper water.

He could foresee serious problems navigating *Hosanna*, using our only remaining engine with an off-centre screw propeller, along the narrow canals especially as she is deep-draughted for the waters that lay ahead. It would have been a slow process even if we still had the more normal centre-line screw; it might well take us twice the time if our vessel had to crab along the canals like a grasshopper with one leg.

We set about seeing if we could get the main engine repaired. We had already spent far too much money on the repair in Milazzo, but at least it had got us this far. We speak tolerable Italian of a general nature, but our technical vocabulary was poor. We had a better knowledge of French and we felt that if we could get through to a good mechanic, we could explain the situation, get an opinion, and see if something could be achieved at moderate expense, bearing in mind our intention of replacing the engine in England, if we ever got there. Our list of Cummins agents in Europe had not produced very valuable results in either Athens or Catania, which were the only times we had had to use it so far, but here we hoped for better things. Lyon was the head office of Cummins in France. That was both good and not so good. Good because the expertise would be there somewhere, bad because it is virtually impossible to penetrate big organisations, which often work on the principle that if you do not already know the name of the person to whom your query should be addressed, you are suspect and should be blocked at all costs from approaching.

Of course the desired headquarters was way out of town. Engineering works usually are. Bill disappeared into the centre of Lyon (he could find no phone boxes near the quay, and few enough anywhere) armed with a phone card and a note book. Of course the number had changed. He had a little linguistic difficulty with the young lady who answered. This too is not unusual.

Though he speaks French quite well, it is only when on the telephone that one realises how much understanding depends on gestures and body language. On the telephone with a frequency pass band so narrow that all the high and low tones of one's speech pattern are cut off too, it becomes quite difficult to follow foreign conversation. The girl did not grasp his French, and he did not understand her English, delightful as it was. Bill tried what he calls The Rude American tack: 'For God's sake honey I'm calling from Minnesota, get me the Service Director.' He got the service director who preferred to speak in French and quickly got the message. 'I will send you a good mechanic to check it out,' he offered, 'Tomorrow.' 'Good.'

Maurice actually turned up at about two the same afternoon, which must be an engineering service record of some sort. Very quickly he dismantled the top of the engine. After various trials he said there was no point in going further: this was a dead engine. Oh yes, it would be quite possible to spend a fortune and having a working engine which would give full power, but it would still be an old engine, and something else could go wrong at any time, et voila! another fortune would have to be thrown at it.

(For the technically minded there were two problems. The Cummins had what are called wet liners. These had corroded, and one was letting water into one cylinder. Cummins also use a unique system of fuel injection. Somehow, in ways that we could not explain, water from the one cylinder had created some sort of back pressure causing surplus fuel that should have returned to the tank to find its way into the neighbouring cylinder through the injector.)

Maurice continued: 'Now we must try to get you home to England. So I go back to the office to see if I can find some spare parts for the old lady, and then tomorrow I return to see what we can do.' 'Yes,' mused Laurel. 'There is one spare part I could do with … only I suppose he means the engine.'

He returned early the next morning, a hot sunny day, which Laurel in old shorts and football shirt was using to get some of the ship's paint freshened up. Maurice said that he was going to put one cylinder out of action, isolate it from all fuel, decompress it, and try to run the engine on five cylinders, or perhaps only four. The surgery will be painful, he added with a smile, but it will not cost much because we keep some old engines for their spares in emergencies. Pleased, we gave him lunch.

At four in the afternoon the engine started and ran on five cylinders. He wanted it to run under load for at least an hour, and this we did, churning up the river while firmly attached to our bollards, while he cleaned up, both himself and the engine, for it had been a dirty job. His van, parked beside us, was impressively fitted with facilities for this, besides containing neat stowage for tools and equipment. This alone gives one confidence. For a while we listened to the thrum of the engine, missing a bit, coughing here and there, but running. We dared to hope.

At about 16.45 the engine died. Nothing, this time nothing, could be done to restart it, and water was getting into one of

the cylinders. '*Le moteur*,' said Maurice, '*est mort sur le table d'intervention*.' (It died on the operating table.)

It would be impossible to fault the service Maurice had performed for us. It was not expensive, and we felt that we had been given the best possible help and advice. Now we knew where we stood. As we shared a cool beer with him we thought of the journey ahead. Maurice was encouraging, the day was fine, and without discussion between us, it seemed to be taken for granted that we would continue. While the voyage was not dangerous, it would not be the doddle that we'd hoped for.

A little yacht *Pipkin II* moored on the quay, flying the RNSA burgee. We got together with her three crew for a beer, and it turned into a jolly wake for our dead engine, which continued on to Le Grenadin for dinner.

We continued the journey north next day, 1 June, after necessary chores and buying bread. Bill went along to the Bureau to pay our canal dues. Navigation on French inland waters used to be free for pleasure craft, but while the numbers of commercial barges have decreased, the number of *plaisanciers* has gone up dramatically and the Canal authorities (*Voies Navigables de France*) had decided to make charges. We were unfortunate as guinea pigs in that to start with they pitched the charges rather unfairly against our sort of boat, but that is the way of things. It would be put right next year, but for the moment we had to pay rather more than seemed just for up to 45 days of navigation, more than sufficient to pass from the Mediterranean to the English Channel. The lady in the office was charmingly helpful. Having calculated the *coquette somme* she cried, 'Oh, La La!' with a wealth of meaning and spent a long while discussing how the total might be reduced. There was a three day 'discovery' licence for 75 francs, she said, could we not get a new one every three days, the difference would be considerable.

Bill however, knows when he is beaten. It was highly unlikely that there would be a Bureau every three days, just when one needed to renew. One can try all sorts of tricks to get round things like this but one is always at the mercy of the authorities. This is not so bad if one can weigh anchor and push off to another country, but with locks on either side one was surrounded by France, and anyway we might want to come back one day. He paid, we placed the document in the wheelhouse window for all to see, and we became legal. We hadn't intended to avoid paying but there was nowhere to do so before Lyon, on the way we had come.

· 7 ·

CREEPING AS WE HAVE SAÔNE

In which we make the Right decision – enter the narrows of the Centre and have trouble with the Left – we go over the top in France

Now we had to decide which route to take north. The Saône is a tributary of the Rhône, and rising far to the north-east it could be expected to be carrying a fair amount of the heavy spring rain that was still flowing down the Rhône valley. This made it desirable to leave the Saône as soon as possible, and this dictated a passage westward through the Canal du Centre which was unknown to us. To have chosen the other route would have meant a hundred kilometres more, say two or three extra days of struggling against an adverse current to reach the Canal de la Marne à la Saône, which we knew well.

In the event we found that even with our new low maximum speed of seven kilometres per hour through the water we could make headway. Slowly we crept northward out of Lyon. Past the kitch and gaudy décor of Paul Bocuse's restaurant at Collonges, which looks as if it escaped from the Golden Mile at Great Yarmouth. Brilliant chef he may be; tasteful decorator he certainly is not. On up the river Saône we went, smaller than the Rhône, but still clearly a river and not a canal.

Considering the late start we did well to arrive at Trévoux, which had no commercial barges at all at the quay as it used to, though the best berth was taken up by a sort of municipal entertainment barge, which was not entertaining at the time. The quay was the kind that makes us sigh: bricked and sloping at a sharp angle. You never know what it is like under water, and can get a nasty surprise. We approached with

69

caution and found it approachable. Sloping banks make it difficult to get from and to the shore. With Laurel being lame we try always to find a good quay. France may furnish parking places for disabled motorists, though they are mostly occupied by perfectly able drivers, but it makes no concessions on the waterways. Boats come under the heading of sport, and by French logic the disabled are *ipso facto* disqualified from sport. Sailing for the disabled is not yet a French concept.

We had a fascinating walk round this lovely small town with its convenient shops and returned on board with our booty. We found a smart motor cruiser, the *Taurimina*, flying the burgee of the Royal Yacht Squadron, circling round anxiously. You can tell an anxious boat: it has a sort of extra flag above its burgee which blows out in the opposite direction. Some people can't see this extra flag. Bill always can, and Royal Yacht Squadron or Bermondsey Boat Club, it makes no difference; someone needs a hand or some advice.

It seemed the owner, who was driving the boat, was a little frail, and wanted a berth where he could land easily, for perfectly reasonable but private reasons. We could have moved, but we too had a disabled person on board, and more important still, we had a long gangway which stretched from our deck to the very top of the awkwardly sloping bank. Clearly it would be better for the old gentleman to land over us, as our two decks were at the same height. We invited him to moor alongside us. This was quickly accomplished, a glass shared, and introductions made, of himself and his two companions.

We were, it seemed, entertaining a Peer of the Realm, a former Speaker of the House of Commons, or rather he was entertaining us for he turned out to be excellent company.

While we went ashore to a good and inexpensive dinner at the Hôtel d'Europe, overlooking the river, our neighbour's party went about their business after we had helped disembark his wheel-chair. On our way back, enjoying the warmth of the evening we came across the intrepid navigator pushing his own wheel-chair back along the tow-path, and clearly in the best of spirits. We all had a drink on board *Taurimina*.

We have notched up quite a good peer count in our wanderings. They are by no means all to be found in gold-plated mega-yachts (*Taurimina* was about 35 feet long and quite modestly but extremely sensibly fitted for a frail owner-driver), but represent a cross section of the total yachting scene. In many cases, one does not become aware of their heraldic precedence until after one has parted company. In our experience, there is little wrong with our peerage that a wider spread of boat ownership could not cure.

Next morning our neighbours left to go downstream and we left upstream; ships that pass in the night and speak to each other in passing.

At breakfast time our generator failed because of overheating, but Bill postponed working on it to make some progress, and we made surprisingly good time as far as Beauregard where our speed over the ground dropped sharply. It was cloudy and cool and the cows were lying down and, sure enough, it began to rain. At Dracé lock there was no keeper, and we had to wait, hooting occasionally, for quite a time before one came running. He avenged the hooting by letting the water into the lock so violently fast that we were thrown about and rolled more than twenty degrees in the surging water. Bill contemplated going after him with the seaman's classic weapon, a belaying pin, a cry of 'Vast there, what be about, ye lubbers!' but fortunately he was persuaded to lose no further time, and we continued on our way in dignified and British silence, and pouring rain.

The downpour continued as at about teatime we berthed alongside the grassy quay at Port Arçiat, with some difficulty as it was very shallow. Monsieur Vaucher the amiable *patron/chef* of the riverside restaurant, the Relais de la Saône, came out under an umbrella to help us moor. The wet spring had produced a luxuriant growth of long meadow grass, and the bollards were completely hidden, so his aid was welcome.

We have described a previous visit by *Hosanna* to this excellent establishment in an earlier book*, when we celebrated two family birthdays with snails en croute and roast sucking pig. Once again we had a splendid meal, though this time our family was not with us to share it. Afterwards we presented the

---

* *Watersteps Through France*

helpful proprietors with the book in which they figured, which was very warmly received. They get little custom from the river nowadays; their clients come from the surrounding towns by car. The faded paint on the gable-end facing the river still informs bargees that they may hold their weddings and *kermesses* here, but it is almost illegible. The days when barges gathered here for a welcome evening of booze and Bal Musette – the French equivalent of a knees-up – are long gone.

Bill got up early to fix the generator (a blocked water filter again) and we were under way at nine. It was sunny and warm, and we reached Mâcon later that morning, where the bridge is looked after by St Nicholas, whose image looks down at you from one of the bridge piers. The best berth at Mâcon town quay was occupied by a Hotel-barge and we had to scramble into the second best (shallow again), to enable Laurel to replenish the fresh provision larder. We had lunch there, then unstuck ourselves with some difficulty, continuing on to Tournus, where it was the same story, but this time we were welcomed alongside the German Hotel-barge *Liberté*. This enabled us to take advantage of a nearby supermarket, which, on a boat, one should always profit from, as convenient ones are rare. While we were there the heavens opened and deluged Tournus with a heavy thunderstorm; nobody left the store while this went on, and conversations struck up among beleaguered customers while waiting, just like the blitz. A fine evening followed, and we dined out again at another favourite: *Les Terraces*, an establishment with more prestige than Monsieur Vaucher's at Arçiat, and an equally good cuisine. This is all wonderful eating country, here in the Lyonnais; why should we not make the most of it?

Bill had been carrying out steering experiments in deep calm water in the big river, to try to predict how *Hosanna* would behave in the canal, which we expected to reach the following day. He found that to maintain a straight course with only the small port engine, he needed about seven degrees of port rudder to counteract the turning moment induced by the off-centre screw.

We were up early the next morning. Our last day on the Saône was cloudy and very cold, we were back to jerseys and

Lauret.

socks. At midday, after passing the last big lock, we reached Chalons-sur-Saône, where we bade farewell to the broad, flowing river and turned into the narrow winding Canal du Centre. It was now lunchtime and the first lock in the canal was closed. The big locks on the rivers Rhône and Saône are run on a commercial basis with the *éclusiers* on shift work, and they stay open late in the evening, even all night, and do not close for lunch. Once you get to the canal where there is not much commercial traffic, the job changes somewhat. The *éclusiers* are on duty long hours and feel justified in ignoring you from twelve thirty to one thirty. You should be having *your* lunch. He arrived on a bike at half past one exactly.

Closing for lunch was not the only difference, now we were in a small canal. Till now, we had been in huge locks with the sides towering many metres above us, and the cats had not liked the smell of slimy concrete, and the echoing noise, and had stayed out of the way. Now the locks were smaller and quiet, and at the top was grass and hedges and twittering birds. As *Hosanna* rose gently, the cats leapt ashore and went for a walk. It took twenty minutes of coax and threaten to get them back. Precautions would have to be taken in future.

Otherwise things had gone well: we had passed this canal lock at the end of a short straight length from the river. We had got there without difficulty and Bill's morale had risen, only to take a sharp tumble when we got further on in the canal.

Even on the straight lengths the amount of rudder needed to maintain a straight course increased to twenty degrees out of a possible forty. Not only did this slow us down, but we found we could not use the full power that even this small engine was capable of. Anything above half speed soon had the ship out of control in the shallow water, and we hit the bank a few times, snapping the staff of our French courtesy ensign among the overhanging trees.

The canal is a very old one, built in the days of towing by horses and thus very slow speeds. It was built on the basic principle of following a contour, and as it is entering hilly country the contours are very curvaceous. It is also evident that the constructors had a warped sense of humour. The bridges are narrow, and virtually every one of them is built on a bend. The locks too, and there are many in the hilly region, are often situated on a right-angled bend. We could manage these well enough if the bend was to the right, but a left hand bend was impossible without stopping to pole ourselves round and into the lock, or landing a rope to pull our head round. It was very wearing. Instead of the two locks a day in the rivers, we had that day done 13, and every one had been a problem, with steering or cats or both. Hitting the bank also gave the cats a chance to escape ashore, and at a time when Laurel's energies were supposed to be directed elsewhere. Sharp words were spoken on the subject, and when we finally made fast for the night at a good berth in Chagny, Bill's morale was near zero and he doubted he had the strength or ability to continue. He had seldom been so low in spirit. Not that *Hosanna* was in any physical danger. Whatever she hit or whatever problems she had in this narrow, shallow canal, we would do it slowly, and were very unlikely not to survive; in fact it was still a good deal safer than travelling by motor-car. His low spirits were caused by professional frustration. He could not manage the boat in these conditions. There was nowhere around with the resources to carry out the major work necessary to replace the main engine. We were trapped. Continuing would be exhausting, but there would be no gain from staying put. We needed a plan.

To emphasise the misery, it was raining and extremely cold, and we lit the wood fire. Warmth and hot food helped.

Bill covered sheets of paper with drawings of the cross-section of the canal with our hull-shape super-imposed, and little arrows representing lines of force sprouting like the straw from a scarecrow. When finally he went to sleep, his last words were that he had found no solution to the problem, which cheerful information caused Laurel to have a sleepless night. She used it to devise theoretical methods of cat control.

Next morning we were faced with a sharp left hand turn if we were to restart our journey. While Laurel prepared a cooked breakfast (she is a firm believer that human endeavour and morale is furthered by food) Bill sat on the foredeck. Eventually he started moving ropes. This was a good sign. Meanwhile Laurel had made modifications to the catflap cupboard. The cats were normally at liberty to come and go through this cupboard, which leads to the verandah. By clamping a piece of wood over the exit, and programming the catflap to 'out but not in' she could imprison a surprised cat or two when life got difficult. She placed a cardboard box in the cupboard, and as soon as we started the engine there was a cat in it, Tansy having attempted her usual route to the dinghy. She settled there quite happily.

Bill carefully explained to Laurel what she should do with the ropes. With the aid of a long spring rope from the boat's shoulders to a bollard on the elbow of the quay, he would work the engine against the rope until the boat turned. Laurel was then to slip the rope and haul it in fast before it got into the screw.

It worked well, but clearly we could not reckon on this lengthy and physically heavy procedure at every left-hand bend. For a start it depended entirely on a suitably placed shore-side bollard, not often present. Morale had improved with the smooth departure and an absence of cats (by this time they were both in the cupboard), but gloom was not far under the surface.

Gradually things improved over the next two days as we learned. Bill found it undesirable to keep *Hosanna* exactly in the middle of the channel, which shallowed close either side of us. The canal is supposed to have an operational depth of 1m 80, but that is theory, and maintenance of this depth depends on continual passages of commercial barges drawing this amount who plough through with powerful engines and push the silt to one side. Our echo-sounders, right forward, reported that the depth was usually between 1m 60 and 1m 70. We are normally 1m 50 deep in the water, and any craft moving over such a slight margin experiences 'squat'; that is to say that the screw draws water from underneath the ship and this sucks her further down into the water. Depending on her speed, this can be as much as 30cm for a boat like *Hosanna*. Hence the limit on our speed through the water, which in turn limited the turning effect of our rudder.

Normally a rudder is helped in producing a turning effect, even in these circumstances, if the thrust stream of the propeller acts directly upon it. We were denied this benefit.

The canal was about 20 metres wide between banks. A section in the middle of about seven metres represented the deeper part, the rest of the bottom sloped upwards until by the banks it was often about 25 cm only. For this reason we had been trying to keep to the centre, extremely difficult on sharp bends.

Bill began to navigate with *Hosanna*, not exactly in the middle but slightly to the right side, so that the left-mounted screw was as near the middle as he could get it. Unfortunately this had the starboard side of the ship rubbing against the shallows on the right-hand side of the canal, and she repeatedly got out of control and sheered off to starboard. Another factor came into play: as a ship moves along a narrow, shallow channel she pushes two wedges of water ahead of her, one either side of her stem. When these wedges are very unequal it makes control that bit more difficult.

By the time we had our elevenses on the third day and had been through several bridges and locks, Bill felt that with no luck in the centre of the channel and no luck over to one side, he was still not entirely in control. When we reached Montchanin that afternoon, we had done only fifty two kilometres since entering the canal three long, hard, nerve-wracking days ago, and had negotiated thirty five locks.

We were at the *partage*, the high point at which we changed from going up the locks to going down. A watershed, literally. Till now, the waters had gone against us, down to the Mediterranean, now five hundred kilometres behind us. From now, the flow would be downhill to the Atlantic or the Channel. In rivers this would be to our advantage, but in canals a lock is much the same work whether you go up or down. The mooring technique changes slightly, as one does not want to leave an eye over a bollard that disappears out of reach above you, and have to climb a slimy ladder to release it. You put the loop over your own bollard, lead the rope round the lock bollard and take a turn with the free end. When the lockgates open, you can either do an impressive flip, or, if that does not work, you can pull the free end round and back on board.

We made fast at the boatyard of Connoisseur Boats Ltd, a company who hire out nice smart cruisers for people to cruise in on their holidays. 'Let's sell this hooker and buy one of those,' said Bill. Clearly we were in need of a rest.

· 8 ·

IT NEVER RAINS BUT IT PALLS

If it rains for St Médard
T'will rain for long and much and hard
(FRENCH PROVERB)

In which we are narrow minded – the Old Ark's
manoeuvrin' all day – dodging the hire boats – the
rains come

The people at the Montchanin boatyard were quite charming, and they offered us electricity and fresh water. The berth was very congenial (grass and trees), the sun shone, and though we took up a good deal of their quay space they made no complaint, as many of their boats were out enjoying themselves. We stopped an extra day, partly because one of the cats was not to be found at departure time. She turned up at midday, but it was too late to make a good start as the next chain of locks was a long one, so we abandoned that day, and used it for constructive leisure: a bit of engine maintenance and grinding off and painting some rusty spots.

The next day we felt we must push on. Bill was surprisingly cheerful after a day of comparative rest. The cats were given no breakfast until after we left in the hope that they would hang about waiting for it, and this strategy did indeed work.

We had gone into the little creek bows first. We now had to back out and turn in a fresh breeze. We did it, running aground only a couple of times, and we were away.

Bill had decided to attempt the middle ground between the two unsuccessful methods he had tried so far, and found to his surprise and delight that it was nearer to a solution. Going along the straights we had little difficulty with the engine at 1100 out of its potential 1800 rpm, even though he estimated that it increased our depth in the water by 20cm. We found that to approach a right hand bend it was better to slow down

79

early, move over to the right side of the deeper part of the channel, and then accelerate round the curve. For the left hand bend, we approached as fast as we dared in the dead centre of the channel, then at the last minute stopped the engine completely and put the rudder hard over. Once or twice it did not work; it would be too late to try to stop by putting the engine astern, and we would plough spectacularly up the right hand bank, necessitating hard work and blasphemy before being able to resume our course again.

We began to have some successes. We also, now the weather was warming up, had another problem to contend with: the hire boats. To start with there had been few on the canal, but we had now reached those parts where the scenery and facilities were attractive to holidaymakers. Not that holidaymakers are unpleasant people, far from it. Nor are they necessarily incompetent; a few are grossly so, but an equal number are at the upper end of the skilful scale. The trouble arises because they fail to appreciate some of the problems peculiar to large barges in small canals.

Leaving a lock for instance: when a barge leaves a lock it effectively fills the gateway. No matter how hard its engine works the water finds it difficult to get past the hull and into the space the barge is vacating behind it. The suction that occurs is the same as when drawing a cork from a bottle. This means that a barge is able to leave a lock only at a very slow speed to start with. During this slow stage its long proboscis, up to 38 metres of it, is thrust out into the canal where it is at the mercy of winds and circulating currents. If a puff of wind blows it to one side, there is nothing at all the barge skipper can do about it except to watch, until finally his stern pops clear of the lock gates. At this point, if he continues with his engine at full throttle, his barge will leap forward (as much as hundreds of tons weight can be said to leap – the term is comparative) in the direction in which it was pointing. If this is not the direction in which he wishes to go, he has either to put his rudder hard over to correct his course, which will make his stern swing violently as he accelerates, or stop his engine and turn gently, assuming he has the room.

Laumel.

On these narrow canals he would have little room. If therefore a barge is leaving and finds that a small pleasure boat is waiting to pass the lock in the opposite direction, and has come up close to the lock gates in eager anticipation like a dog waiting for the kitchen door to open, the barge cannot correct his course because his swinging stern would demolish the pleasure boat, and he is condemned therefore to go up the bank.

We experienced this problem several times, exacerbated in our case by our inability to turn to port. In vain Bill would ask the waiting pleasure boats to stay well back. It is THE CORRECT THING TO DO in any event. Some professional barge skippers are able to find eloquent words to express their deep appreciation of a pleasureboat's desire to snuggle up at the exit of a lock.

It is slightly different if a barge is waiting for a lock. If you really want to hear barge language at its most inventive, just try to nip ahead of one into a lock. The barge cannot manoeuvre in the canal, or hold still, and it is necessary in a wind for him to creep slowly forward all the time. This does bring him up to the lock gates on occasions, and in this case he will usually make fast on the *patte d'oie*, or goose foot, a wooden structure which also helps to fair a barge into the lock. Such is the construction of barges, straightsided and with no projections, that it is quite acceptable for the barge leaving the lock to slide gently along the side of the barge waiting. For obvious reasons he cannot do that with a yacht. It is worth pointing out that a barge leaving a lock will suck sideways into any craft that it passes, particularly while it is accelerating. For all these reasons it is best to keep 100 metres away from a lock, rising or falling, until you are sure it is empty. Getting a green light does not mean that the lock is unoccupied.

The other problems with the hire craft were mostly concerned with their tendency to do unexpected and even dangerous things at no notice at all. Drivers who in a car would not dream of changing lanes without signalling to the vehicles behind happily do this in a boat, forgetting that a ship has no brakes, and we cannot stop a hundred tons in a few metres, no matter how slowly we are going. Anyone cutting across the bows of a bigger craft takes an unjustifiable risk.

Bill does not enjoy the prospect of collision, but there is no point putting one's own craft into difficulties by taking avoiding action that has no possibility of being effective in time. It merely increases tension. One ploughs on regardless at one's steady 5 kilometres per hour (about 3 mph) and hopes for the much more manoeuvrable hire boats to get their act in order and out of our way.

All in all, driving on the Canal du Centre was at doctorate level and Bill had to do most of it. There were a few straight stretches where Laurel could take the wheel and give him a break. Sometimes she ran aground. As he admitted, generously, running aground or up the bank was par for the course, whichever of us was driving.

We had to wait for the swing bridge at Montceau-les-Mines. It was the sacred lunchtime. Virtually on the stroke of noon, throughout the whole of France the vista is of a country cleared of people as if depopulated by the plague. Mad dogs and Englishmen go out in the midday sun maybe, but ravenously hungry Frenchmen get their feet in the midday trough.

Of course there were no bollards to make fast to while waiting, but the municipality had put some very pretty railings round a very fine car-park, all decorated with beautiful flower beds, and we made fast to these railings. It is remarkable how municipalities, who spend fortunes on providing elegant and elaborate car parking for those tourists who arrive by road, provide nothing for, even in many cases hindering, those of us who arrive by water.

We had our lunch while stopped. Laurel had fashioned a long lead for the more adventurous cat, so that if it did hop ashore she knew which flowerbed it was in. It was quite a pleasant spot. We could not help contrasting our own mining towns with this one. Bill's maternal family comes from the mining area of the Nottinghamshire, Derbyshire, West Riding contiguation, and it has to be said that town centres in that area were, in his young days, not exactly beautiful. Montceau-les-Mines had a clean and cared for look.

The bridge started to open before we had finished lunch. We swallowed our mouthfuls, grabbed our cat and made ready. The *pontiers* of France decide when boats shall pass.

During the afternoon we ran into further difficulties. The canal became more sinuous and the crumbling banks were even less well maintained. The wind steadily increased until ship-handling at low speed became very difficult and there were problems with number 10 lock. Apparently some pleasure boats had got into trouble at number 11, and it required personnel reinforcements to sort it out. While waiting for the *éclusier* to return, we had to try to make fast to a bank we could not even approach for shallows.

The keeper, when he returned, was scathing about the *plaisanciers* in the other lock. They had got three boats into the lock together, which is quite normal, and had then succeeded in getting them jammed in, which is not. One of the boats had been French, and the *éclusier* had emptied his vocabulary on them because he was better able to express his not inconsiderable feelings adequately. The French lady on board had burst into tears, an excellent way of winning the argument, and the *monsieur* had then become belligerent; obviously the *éclusier* felt that it had been a jolly good party.

Over to the westward beyond a line of poplars as straight as a row of Guardsmen, the sky was darkening to bruise purple as the day ended. We had done fifteen locks, a record for this trip, and had two groundings, one of which had entailed warping ourselves off with the capstan. It was now six thirty and we felt it was time to stop. In the twenty minutes it took us to find an approachable bank, the threatened storm was upon us with surprising suddenness. Thunder crashed all round and we could see the lightning touching base in the fields; the wind rose to storm force and the hissing rain had that tropical intensity that one seldom feels in England, and in which it seems that one is almost immersed in the liquid. In these conditions we came up to our mooring at Génélard.

Laurel has the only effective oilskin we carry. Guess who stays in the wheelhouse exercising command while she gets wet on the foredeck. To be fair, Bill has been trying to buy an oilskin coat that comes down to his knees ever since his old naval one became too stiff to bend round the corners and developed a reek that caused maggot breeders to faint. Such garments used to be common. Nowadays, oilskins for sailors have become part of the fashion trade. One has only to visit the stands of the makers at the Boat Show to have this made abundantly clear. Protective clothing needs a second mortgage to buy and either has the technical complexity of a deep-sea diving suit requiring a full half hour to don or remove and the assistance of an expert dresser, or else it is a light and whimsical outfit in startling colours made to be worn in marina bars by young men who rapidly tear its pockets with their Filofaxes. All these garments stop short of a tall man's genitals. What Bill is searching for is a simple knee-length coat with a high collar, like the old black Pusser's oilskin he had in the Royal Navy, colour not an issue, but preferably *not* pink or purple. Someone, somewhere, must still be making sensible gear. It was to be another year before he succeeded in finding one.

In the meantime he felt that there was no point in being Captain if you ended up wetter than the crew. Laurel's comments on the whole thing were unladylike. It is a long running saga. *A suivre* as the French say (to be continued).

Meanwhile, it was Laurel who stood in the downpour with a rope in her hand.

On this occasion we had more than usual difficulty approaching the bank and getting our mooring ropes on the only two bollards in sight, which were well back from the edge. We were in the shallows again. The grassy bank was at best a good four feet from the ship, it was muddy and slippery, Laurel is lame. Even with the Grannypole to aid her (this is a six foot galvanised pole mounted vertically when needed between the two for'ard bollards; it steadies the person jumping ashore or climbing up to reach a high wharf and is invaluable) the gap was too wide to jump. It looked as if Bill would have to face up to the deluge.

It is not certain whether Laurel's face was covered in tears of frustration or drops of rainwater. She hates to fail and never uses her disability as an excuse, but we have to be realistic and leaping about like this is not her forte.

Bill was saved at the bell by the welcome appearance of a manifestation of pure delight. It is not often that a man in distress is saved by a damsel. But splashing along the bank, or rather hopping from tuft to tuft in the rough grass came an apparition consisting of an oilskin jacket on bare legs. From the shape of the legs (and Bill being under cover had the leisure to notice these things), the apparition was female.

The kind fairy took our ropes, slipped the eyes over the bollards on shore and sensibly disappeared at speed back to a neighbouring barge we could dimly discern through the sheeting rain. We then inched ourselves into position as best we could, and in spite of his best efforts Bill ended up almost as wet as Laurel. She was a little acid about the situation. Diluted acid, of course.

The rain continued very heavy all evening and we deferred a visit to our benefactor to express gratitude. Laurel made a warming oxtail stew with dumplings, which we lubricated with a bottle of lusty Cahors *Etiquette Noir*; just the thing for such a night. We turned in early.

During the night Bill had a severe attack of asthma, the first for many years.

Before we lived in a boat, when Bill had a normal sort of job, he had frequent attacks of asthma as well as severe bronchitis. They were bad enough to be one of the principal reasons for his early retirement. As soon as we passed down channel on our maiden voyage to Gibraltar the asthma disappeared. He had never had another attack since, and we think that alone is a remarkable endorsement of our way of life. Now we had to ask ourselves, what had made the problem recur? Since leaving the broad river, we were now well and truly among the fields, and the hay fever season had started. Bill had already suffered a little.

It is also true that just before bedtime, one of the cats, who had also had a bad day, had chosen to sit on his chest in an unusual display of affection. Bill is not all that fond of cats and generally they are well aware of it, but on this occasion he was rather touched by the purring warm bundle under his neck, though he complained that he sensed irritation in the throat. Was this the cause? Was it even a factor? It had never been in the past. Or was the attack caused by the considerable increase in tension that had also taken place since we entered the canal, and had the cat's fur been merely a trigger? It would take a person with much more knowledge than we have to come to any conclusion and, even then, given the present state of research into this debilitating malady, it would most likely be the wrong one. In the event, attacks of asthma were to continue spasmodically for the next month or two whether or not he had been catsat, and were often related to thunderstorms.

Having had no asthma at all to deal with for so long, we had no treatment to hand and we both had an appalling night, one suffering and the other worrying. We were in no condition to continue next day. Laurel was writing up the log. 'Do you realise what day it was yesterday?' she asked.

'Fifteen locks, a thunderstorm and an attack of asthma – Black Wednesday, I should think,' said Bill morosely.

'It was June the Eighth, St Médard,' said Laurel. We'd lived in Provence, we knew what that meant. St Médard in France is like St Swithin's in England. If the old adage held true we were in for forty days of rain. Great.

To cheer ourselves up we went to call our neighbours in *Golden Thistle* to thank them for their help; it had been a service well beyond the call of duty. 'It's Douglas you should thank,' said Jean. 'It was his attack of conscience that drove me out to help you.' We did not ask if she had the only oilskin.

We were rapt by the elegance of *Golden Thistle*, a converted Dutchman like *Hosanna*, though of a different breed. She was immaculate, she was beautiful, she was exquisitely painted, inside and out, and put our travel-weary home to shame. Her owners, the family Draycott, had read our previous books and having accepted our thanks went quite over the top by inviting us to lunch. We had so many things of common interest to discuss that lunch continued until five o'clock and then later we joined them for a simple dinner at the little restaurant L'Entracte, by the lock. Simple is the right word. It is not as the guides would say worth a detour; indeed it is not worth much of an effort at all, though anything is enjoyable in the right company. While we were out both cats had been stocking up their personal larders with fieldmice they had slaughtered in the grassy banks of the canal.

Much recovered and with morale restored, we parted company with *Golden Thistle* who was southbound. We locked through northbound. We noticed that there were much better moorings on the northernmost side of the lock, where, of course, we were not now going to stop. Such is life. But if we had gone on through the lock that rainy evening, we'd have missed meeting *Golden Thistle* and that would have been a sad loss.

For 10 June it was a cold grey day with a temperature in the fifties (sorry, we have never adapted to the insensitive centigrade scale and consider it too late now to try. We will however continue our efforts to become masters of the metre), and we longed for some of the Greek sunshine we had left behind in April. The day turned out to be another less than successful experience.

First we grounded by the entrance to a lock and took over a quarter of an hour to get off, finally warping ourselves clear with a very long rope to the lock using our power capstan, not a simple task for the two of us. Then Bill made an error of judgement rounding a bend, a right-hand one too, which meant that we were accelerating to full speed as we became aware that all was not well. Up the bank we went, and this time we were well on. For half an hour we laboured, trying to shove off with a quant pole which finally broke.

We paused for a rest and a short indulgence in despair, when we heard two youthful distant voices piping in unmistakeably English tones. Two young people were cycling along the tow path on the opposite side of the canal.

'Hey!' called Laurel, with brilliant inspiration, 'Where's your Dad?'

Dad was following along with the catamaran, they said. Whoopee.

Meantime, Bill had the idea that he could throw a light rope across to the children, that they could be asked to use that as a messenger to haul over a heavy one and make it fast to a tree, and then we would be able to haul ourselves off with the hydraulic capstan. Bill can throw a rope a long way; indeed he prides himself on this skill, but against the wind his throw could not quite reach the opposite bank.

At that moment the catamaran *Hoppercat* rounded the bend. We first had to wait for a commercial barge to pass, and then it took no time at all for a 25 mm diameter rope to be passed across the canal via *Hoppercat* and fastened to a tree, and we were able to haul ourselves off. The Good Samaritans helped us disentangle the bits and pieces and, bearing our grateful thanks, they re-embarked their young and their bicycles, since the ride and the adventure had let off sufficient steam, and went on their way southbound. *Bon voyage*!

Next stop Digoin, after an eleven lock day. A few French municipalities have done things to help the boating fraternity. Some have been very public spirited (Arles comes to mind) while others have allowed a thoroughly commercial enterprise to set itself up, sometimes, we suspect, for the benefit of a friend of the mayor. We do not know whether or not the Base Nautique at Digoin is the result of such machinations. A number of moorings had been provided, mostly with quite superfluous facilities, and at a high price. These had been architect-designed to look gorgeous on the Artist's Impression, but the finished details were crafted (we are sure that is the word they would use) by someone who did not understand boats in any way. Mooring rings were badly placed, and large bushes had been planted right at the quay's edge where their branches prevented boats actually lying against the quays. We tried to moor and found that in the only position a boat of our size could occupy, our wheelhouse had been invaded by a belligerent pine tree, which was aggressively dropping needles all over the chart table. 'Just like Christmas,' said Laurel, trying to beat the branches back through the side door, 'and weather to match.' It was again pouring with rain and bitterly cold. We fought the pine tree out of the wheelhouse and slammed the door. Laurel gave up the pretence of summer and cooked more oxtail stew and dumplings.

Laurel has long known that when Bill becomes emotional the best prescription is oxtail and dumplings. It was looking increasingly likely that by the time we got to Calais we would have started a new breed of French Manx Cattle.

· 9 ·

NO TIME FOR COMPLAINTS

A stitch in time saves nine,
But a stitch in hand was not what we planned.
(VARIATION ON A PROVERB)

In which we meet a retired marinier – wounds and
worse – gastronomic hospitality – under the bridges of
Paris – the working mariniers

Next morning, on our return from a shopping trip, we were accosted by a man who advised us that there was a better (and free) mooring further on.

Such benefactors must be acknowledged. We invited the gentleman on board to find he was a retired *marinier* who lived close by and whose house was a *de facto* museum of the French canals. Come and see, he said. We spent a very informative noontide being told of the implements and tools of his trade. His wife, engaged in giving two foster children their lunch, hospitably filled our glasses. His pride and joy, which we had to admire, was a huge, completed jigsaw puzzle of an unidentifiable naval battle of the Nelsonic period, probably one of the few the French won, and which had been varnished and framed to occupy a large part of his living room wall. Down the garden were tillers, winches, barge poles, and weathercocks, lovingly restored. We would have liked to stay longer, but did not wish to intrude on their lunch. We moved to the free berth and later dined ashore at a small restaurant near the bridge. It was not memorable.

One gets little idea in the canal at Digoin of the town's very handsome frontage to the river Loire, which we discovered on our evening walk. The broad reaches were peaceful now, but with all the evidence of the river's lapses from good behaviour: boulders and tree trunks cast up on mid-stream sandbanks. Mooring rings high up the *levées* showed that once this river flooded and was used for commerce. Now there is none.

As one leaves Digoin the canal crosses the Loire on a spectacular aqueduct. It presented us with no problems of boat management as it was so narrow that there was no question even of steering, and with the motor in slow ahead we advanced as if on tramlines. It was a very odd experience to look down and see the river Loire flowing some 30 feet below. We had an illusion of sailing downhill. We are so used to the assumption that the surface of the water is absolutely level that when the planes of the surroundings create such an optical illusion, the brain will not accept it and creates its own explanation.

After crossing the river by aqueduct, the Canal du Centre ended and became the Canal Latéral à la Loire. Nothing much else changed: it was still narrow and twisty. We started on a winding section heading in a general north-westerly direction. It was hard going again, needing high concentration, and we stopped for lunch at Pierrefitte. Things improved after lunch and we made better progress until teatime when *Hosanna* took the ground quite hard. She seemed to choose teatime for this and it was inevitably the harbinger of a blackening sky and the mooring-up thunderstorm. This duly upset our mooring procedures and we both got wet. It wasn't as if it was a good place to stop, Garnat-sur-Engievre, but we'd done 39 kilometres and nine locks, and it felt like enough. We walked into the town for a change of scene; it had nothing, not even a café.

Deçize was our next stop after only 25 kilometres and six locks, on a day when the going had been easier, and Laurel had been able to take over quite a bit of the driving. There was an Intermarché where we could purchase some stores, but it was a Monday and everyone was fasting; all the restaurants were closed.

At Le Guétin there is another aqueduct, or *pont-canal,* followed by a good basin where it would be a delight to moor for the night if it were possible to approach the bank. It is all silted up, but we managed to get our bows, drawing a mere metre, within about three metres of the bank and were then able to cross to the shore on our long gangway. It had been a good day, we had done all of forty two kilometres and only seven locks, so we dined out at the Auberge du Pont-Canal, quite good, but surprisingly empty. This was mid June, in a pleasant waterside restaurant, and only three tables were occupied.

In the morning early we were asked to move as gentlemen with hard hats and striped poles swarmed over the bank setting up their little things on tripods and calling out to each other across the basin. They were surveying with a view to dredging and we had no wish to discourage them. We arrived at lunchtime at the establishment of the English family Watson at Poids de Fer, recommended by *Golden Thistle*. Here we were determined to have a short break, as we were now halfway up France.

Though the French have now woken up to the pleasure potential of their lovely canals, it was the English who jolted them out of their slumber. Families such as the Watsons managed to get concessions to moor a few boats and set up a gardiennage business, looking after private boats whose owners can only use them for part of the year. Though no-one supposes that they make a fortune, they have the pleasure of a lovely bankside house with a fine garden and are hospitable hosts to passers-by. It must be a pleasant mode of life. We berthed at a grassy quay, with a wooded slope up to the house. The weather became warm and sunny, and the daily teatime thunderstorm ceased for a few days. Both we and the cats relaxed.

We had arranged to pick up mail there. Always one of the biggest problems for travellers, it is doubly so for canal folk, for one never knows within a little what timetable one can keep. We move at walking speed and the world no longer understands such a modest rate of progress. While waiting, we painted and varnished, and got out the sewing machine to recover the verandah bench cushions, hoping to have more of our meals out there as the weather improved.

When the mail arrived we pressed on to stop at St Satur, after nine locks and 38 kilometres. It had become very warm, and we dined in the St Roch restaurant to celebrate our hundredth lock since the Mediterranean. St Roch (dog bites and plague) has a chapel for *mariniers* in the town. The restaurant named after him was constructed over two barges of a type known as *flûtes* from the Canal du Berry, moored together like a catamaran on the banks of the Loire, alongside which, as its name tells, our canal was running. It was a lovely evening, the river looked beautiful, there were children paddling in the shallows, the food was good, and the restaurateurs hospitable. But the restaurant, which we had expected to be full, was virtually empty. Evidently they were having a bad season hereabouts. France was in recession.

19 June was not a good day at all. To start with Bill woke to a chesty cold, and for a person liable to bronchitis that is a bad omen. Normally we might have stopped for a day or two to see how things developed, but Bill wanted to press on. Fate, however, had it in for us.

There were plastic bags in the intakes for the cooling water. This is a perennial problem for boats in general owing to the incurable habit that the world's population has of getting rid of these convenient wrappings by throwing them into the water. The problem is generally as bad as the tendency for the local supermarkets to offer unlimited plastic bags to their customers. In the USA for example, where environmental matters were high on the agenda, the supermarkets packed one's purchases in large, strong, degradable paper bags. These do not cause pollution, but on the other hand, while fine for those who can transfer the bags straight from supermarket trolley to the boot of a car, they are a bit too degradable for boat people. They have no handles, and when one dumps them into a dinghy whose bottomboards are usually damp, one has to row fast for one's boat before the moisture reduces them to pulp and one's purchases debouch all over the floor.

In Italy, where plastic bags are virtually thrown at one (perhaps because they are charged for), the situation is so bad that some harbours have a floating scum of plastic bags almost thick enough to walk on. In places this scum extends fully out to the limit of Italian territorial waters. It is almost as bad on the French coast, with the added hazard of empty plastic mineral water bottles floating high out of the water and scooting about in puffs of wind like water-boatmen insects on the village pond.

It is possible to arrange a boat's engines so as not to have to pump water from outside in order to cool the cylinders, sucking in foreign bodies with it. Many canal boats have a different system with a continuous enclosed water cycle, but then they cannot pump the used cooling water into the exhaust where it would act as an efficient silencer. Trouble-free cooling and noisy exhaust, or the other way round. Nothing is perfect.

After dismantling and cleaning the filters, we found one of the lock-keepers having his own personal strike. He had been abused by a *plaisancier* and was sulking. We sat there with our bows up his lock gates until he had finished a long lunch and recovered his sang-froid. Bill heard a long recital of the problems of a lock-keeper. He was not sympathetic. He felt the surly lock-keeper had probably asked for trouble, but Bill maintained the British reputation for calm and perhaps eased the path of coming navigators with occasional murmurs of '*C'est vrai?*', or '*Ca m'étonne*', or even on one occasion '*C'est pas possible*' ('*Mais si, Monsieur*').

The next lock-keeper was by contrast cheerful and helpful. He had an incentive. By the lock he kept a shed full of wines for sale by the case to passing boats. We bought a case of very good Sancerre at a fair price, perhaps the only enlightenment of the day, for wine is a heavy product to carry to one's boat when there is no personal transport.

It was a standard day, 38 kilometres, slightly fewer than average locks (five), and the usual teatime thunderstorm to coincide with berthing at a good quay miles from anywhere. Bill felt unwell and collapsed damply into his armchair while the cat leapt on his chest. Within minutes he was having a very severe attack of asthma again and was in considerable distress. He decided to go for a walk; it had stopped raining for a time and he felt the clean local air, free of cats, might be beneficial.

He walked into the nearby village, about a kilometre, trying hard to suck in quantities of good air, but he had little success and turned back. Coming back was uphill and he was soon in serious trouble. He had to sit on the ground by the roadside gasping for breath for nearly half an hour, while the rain restarted. Laurel, concerned at his failure to re-appear, set out to look for him, but she saw him coming along the tow-path, not exactly staggering, but walking like an old man, unrecognisable from his usual military gait.

He went to bed early, tranquillized, and started a course of antibiotics.

Our fortunes did not improve the next day. Bill's bronchitis was worse, but he insisted that we move on; he didn't like the berth. So while Bill sat wrapped in wool at the back of the wheelhouse, Laurel drove out of the Canal Latéral à la Loire, into the Canal de Briare.

We had more trouble with the cooling water filters, which Bill had to see to. We crossed the famous aqueduct of Briare, but were too preoccupied to appreciate its beauty. The sides of the aqueduct channel were breaking away leaving bolt-heads and bent steel angles protruding from the wooden piles, and *Hosanna* needed delicate handling to avoid damage, it being impossible to use fenders because they caught on the projections.

After the town of Briare we started to climb again out of the Loire valley, Laurel still driving. She had a few bad experiences, going up the bank a couple of times, and having trouble recovering, not wanting to further disturb her invalid. Bill tried to rest on the wheelhouse bench, occasionally offering a bit of advice.

Suddenly the tables were turned.

In lock number 12, we were just making ready to start again when Laurel observed one of the cats, feeling friendly and about to leap on the Bill's chest. She made a desperate effort to stop it, fearing more asthma attacks, and caught the back of her hand against the corner of the underside of the table, splitting the skin. It was a jagged wound and would need stitching. She cleaned it and bound it up, but Bill had perforce to drive. There were six more locks to pass before the village of Rogny, where the lock-keepers told us was the nearest doctor, and his surgery was close to the quay. As Laurel could no longer tend the lines, we gave up mooring in the locks, and Bill held the boat in place with the engine. It took his mind off his own troubles. Fortunately the quay at Rogny was easy to approach and moor to. While Bill made fast, Laurel went off in search of the doctor, whose surgery in fact fronted the quay.

Bill followed on to the surgery. There was a short wait for the doctor's arrival. By common consent, the queue that was already there compassionately allowed Laurel to go first (it is very important to bleed in the waiting room), and after a shout or two, Laurel emerged, stitched, bandaged and reassured. 'It's the hand I draw with,' she told the doctor. 'Don't be anxious, it will be as good as new,' he said.

All the same, as we returned to the boat, we were both miserable, fed up and tired. We had done 14 locks and only 16 kilometres. We were never going to finish our journey.

Did anybody want to buy a barge?

It was in this condition that we met on the quayside a pleasant young man walking his dog. He was most sympathetic and turned out to be the chef/proprietor of the nearby Auberge des Sept Ecluses; it being Monday his restaurant was closed. Never mind, he said, I will open just for you. You do not want to cook with your hand in bandages. In fact several other people took advantage of his Monday opening. We had an excellent dinner and morale began to rise again. This young man is a remarkable chef. We decided to rest a further day and invited Laurent, our chef, and Emmanuelle, his wife, on board the barge.

Laurent, who had been the assistant chef in the Elysée Palace, the official residence of the President of France, was fascinated by Laurel's vast collection of Indian and far Eastern spices. We both love curries and Malayan dishes (Bill served out there in the days of Empire), and spicy Turkish mixtures for *köfte* (meatballs), and Laurent was keen to learn, for in France the art of good Middle East and Indian cookery is unknown, though there are many Vietnamese restaurants. Laurent and Laurel poked in jars and pots, tasting and talking excitedly. She gave him several samples, and he insisted we return for dinner at the restaurant, not as customers this time, but as his guests. He would close the restaurant, he said, he wanted to try these spices. We also keep a large stock of chutney, as it often makes a useful present for ex-pats, and we gave him two jars.

Seven o'clock found us in the kitchen of the Auberge. Together Laurel and Laurent cooked curried lamb. Our contributions were the various spices, some *raita* (yoghurt, mint and cucumber), some creamed coconut and poppadoms, and of course the mango chutney. We were impressed with the open mind of this very young chef and his skill in handling his material. The curry was good, we all enjoyed it, agreeing however that it might have been better if made the day before,

when the spices would have had more time to penetrate the other ingredients.

When it came to dessert, we chose *crême brulée*, and were very glad we did. We watched him take the white china dishes containing the *crême* from the fridge, carefully sprinkling the tops evenly with brown sugar. We then watched with delighted amazement as he took from a cupboard a blowlamp, lit it and proceeded to caramelise the sugar with this humdrum DIY tool. He grinned at the expression on our faces. '*Voilà*,' he said, 'now you know the secret of *crême brulée*.' It was a far cry from the crême caramel of the average tourist menu. It was creamy, fine textured and cool, and by contrast the caramel top was deliciously crackly, like sherry-coloured ice.

'Did any customers want to eat at the restaurant tonight?' we asked, feeling a little guilty at monopolising the kitchen. Laurent's grin got even wider. 'I turned away six Germans,' he said. 'But I am not sorry. Life should not be all work and we have enjoyed ourselves.'

We wish them well and expect to see Laurent's name honoured in his own country one day.

Bill's chest was a little better when we left the next day. Laurel, though healing well, was unable to handle any mooring ropes, so we left ourselves free in the locks. We learned some new skills, one or other of us using the engine to hold the boat roughly in place as the water surged about us. It was a cold and cloudy day, bringing our winter clothing out of its drawers again, and we were glad to moor up at Amilly to a disused oil station quay after the fourteenth lock of the day. Laurel did not feel like cooking, neither did Bill, and we patronised the smart restaurant overlooking the lock. We had a very good dinner there, not quite the only diners, but it was not cheap, and the atmosphere was coolly formal. It was a marked contrast to the friendliness of Laurent at the Auberge des Sept Ecluses. The cooking was roughly equivalent in skill, but at the Auberge de l'Ecluse at Amilly, one felt one was worshipping at the shrine of Haute Cuisine. Life *was* all work, and one was not there to enjoy oneself.

Perhaps it was because we were not ourselves on top form. We were cross-grained all next day too, after a bad beginning: the engine failed to start. We spent half an hour on useless remedies before noticing that the stop lever on the dashboard had been left in the up position. As soon as this was put right the engine started sweetly as usual. It was hard to avoid one of those 'and-whose-fault-was-*that*' inquests.

Other minor events were exacerbated by our own lack of well-being, retrieving reluctant cats from an exciting rubbish dump for instance, though Bill's bronchitis was responding to the antibiotics. We have to worry about this because his recovery potential depends on where the belligerent bug was obtained. In Greece, antibiotics are available over the counter without prescription, and are taken without medical advice, like throat lozenges. People therefore tend to economise and discontinue the course when they start to feel better, and this leads to a build-up of a resistance to antibiotics in the local germ population. A dose of bronchitis which responds to a course of 250 mg tetracycline in England, needs blasting with 500 mg ammunition in Greece. If this bug had been a Greek one which had been lying dormant for a month or two, Bill could have been in trouble.

It appeared to be a French germ, responding to normal doses, but it had left him weak and tetchy. During the day we left the Canal de Briare, and entered the Canal de Loing. It was a fifteen lock day, and to end it we had a difficult moor under some trees at Nemours. Bill went for a walk to try to buy hydraulic oil. He recorded in the log: 'Walked through town. Big, brutally noisy fairground at far end. Everywhere closed. The town is a dump.' He is inclined to express his feelings, but he does not usually feel quite so negative. No oil was available.

In these circumstances it was a relief to calm down and recall that this was the part of the world beloved by Alfred Sisley, who painted the river and Canal de Loing all his life, for the last twenty years of which he lived at Moret-sur-Loing. He painted light and sky and water, and the water as a mirror to the sky, and like the other Impressionist painters was painfully poor during his lifetime, unable to sell pictures that almost the day he died began the climb in value to the multi-thousands of pounds they cost today.

We reached St Mammès next day, soon after lunch. It was very hot. St Mammès is a busy barge port, at the confluence of the Canal de Loing and the rivers Yonne and Seine. We thought that here we would find what we needed: oil, provisions and cash. The oil was easy. A new fuelling station run by helpful and good mannered folk was on the opposite bank, and they had everything we wanted for the boat in stock at a fair price. A good start.

The cash was another matter. St Mammès has no bank, and tomorrow was Saturday. It was now or never. Never mind, said our information source, drawing on his Gauloise, there is a bank on the other side of the river Seine. Cross the bridge, and go up the hill and you will find the town of Champagne-sur-Seine, it's only a kilometre.

In Greece one gets used to people under-estimating distances. If it is a four kilometre walk to the nearest whatever-it-is then your kind, considerate Greek will assure you it is only a kilometre – 'Two cigarettes away'. He does not want to discourage you. He wants you to feel good. But Bill did not expect to find the cigarettes so long in France. He is, however, dogged. He set out to find cash and he walked for 50 minutes before he came to the town with a bank. He got his money, walked back and went early to bed.

After getting our oil we had moored, with permission, outside four commercial barges, one retired and three awaiting cargoes. On Saturday morning it was pouring with rain and we had to get provisions. Next to us in the barge *Eglantine* were a young couple who told us that the supermarket was quite a long way and offered to take us in their car. We accepted with heartfelt gratitude and climbed into their middle aged but serviceable Renault. The supermarket had the appearance of having been stripped by locusts, due to yesterday's sudden heat, which had blown all the freezers, and the whole store was about to shut down for repairs. Naturally there were some bargains to be had and we managed to find the essentials at little cost, including some New Zealand lamb which Laurel roasted, English style, that evening. Getting the stores, including several crates of beer against hot days, across the decks of four barges would have been almost impossible but for the help of *Eglantine*, and by the time we had finished we were very tired. Bill slept all afternoon.

There was a big market on the quayside on the Sunday morning. Laurel loves markets and we delayed departure for half an hour to indulge her. She supplemented yesterday's hastily collected basics with the fresh fruit and vegetables that are so good in the open air markets of France, and some pork liver for the cats.

Then we left on an easy passage, with only six locks in the river Seine to Alfortville in the southern suburbs of Paris. On the way we had time to realise that we had discovered nothing about St Mammès. He did not appear among the *mariniers'* saints. Who was he and how did he give his name to the town? We are still trying to find out. We would also like to know what wag aptly called the old railway bridge at Melun the Devil's Fart Bridge.

Alfortville was not salubrious. We moored to a high wall edged by a narrow brick path which led up steps to the main road. Bill went for a walk to see the lie of the land. He returned to say that a huge flea-market was packing up, but that he did not recommend fraternisation with the inhabitants. The surrounding buildings were HLMs (*Habitation à Location Moyenne*), or what we would call council flats, very high rise. The area was decidedly scruffy. He saw very few persons that he could describe as being of European origin. We were glad that the boat was invisible from the road, and decided to shut down the hatches and keep the cats on board. Apart from the main road just up an alluring flight of steps, Bill thought the locals would probably eat a fat cat if they caught one. He felt lucky to have got back safely himself. We have to face facts. Unemployment in the larger French cities is far worse among the immigrant population; the French press are frank, nay, specific, about the racial origins of criminals, and the statistics of crime according to racial origin are collated and published. They do not make comfortable reading. Nevertheless, our night at Alfortville was untroubled.

The Seine was flowing strongly under us the next morning, the recent thunderstorms having caused some flooding upstream. The lock above which we had moored the night before was called, appropriately, the Port a L'Anglais (the English Gate), quite the right one for us to begin the day's journey through Paris.

It was a lovely day and we decided to start early. Only two kilometres on our way we came to the confluence of the Marne, coming in from our right, and suddenly we were in what seemed like an oriental Disneyland. The point of land dividing the two rivers was entirely Chinese: pagodas, buildings with curved corners to their emerald roofs to send the demons flying, moongates and stone lanterns. It was the Chinagora Centre, including the Motel and Restaurant Guangdong. We could not see anywhere in the complex a quay for customers coming by water, with or without a junk, or we might have been tempted to stop for lunch. The combination of French produce and Chinese cooking was a beguiling thought, but we tore our eyes from the exotic sight to make sure nothing was coming down the Marne, and escaped towards the City.

Coming to Paris by car, as we often have done, one goes round the City by the Périphérique and, if you are heading for Calais, you cross the Seine eastbound at Ivry. That terrible Ring Road, thunderously overburdened and thick with exhaust, panic, and imprecation, was over our heads now, and causing us no pain at all. The Seine was quiet, there was little traffic on the river, the Bateaux-Mouches had not begun the day's work of posting parcels of neatly packaged tourists from here to there, but above us was the faint hum of a highway choking to death as the citizens of Paris drove to work. We did not envy them.

Paris is thick with history and the Seine running through it is the silver thread that links the centuries. In the far off mists of time, Bacchus, God of wine, had a lovely daughter, the nymph Sequana, who came on a visit to Ceres, Goddess of Agriculture. Ceres lived, how could it be otherwise, among the rich cornfields of Gaul. Neptune took a fancy to the nymph, and rising from the sea put out what must have been a long and salty arm and seized her by her veil. Loudly she cried for help, and her father and her protectress both came to her aid, tearing the veil. Nymph and veil dissolved into water drops, and became the source of the Seine. (So many nymphs unfortunate enough to attract the attention of some philandering deity suffered transmogrification to save their honour; one wonders that the supply of nymphs did not run out.) The Gallo-Romans left us this legend, paddling their wooden dugouts across the river which was their High Street, inter-village road, communications network, and defence against enemies. Traffic on the waters of the Seine is thousands of years old; only the boats have changed.

When Caesar's legions arrived 50 years before the birth of Christ, they found a swampy island in the river Seine, inhabited by a tribe who took to boats almost before they

Launet.

learned to walk. It was at the intersection of two routes, one
from the Rhinelands going south to the cornfields and vineyards, this island being the most easily forded point on the
river. The other route was the river itself, so much easier and
quicker for trade and barter and communication than even a
Roman road. The Romans, in their usual high-handed fashion,
called the *place Lutetia*, and burned the two wooden bridges

that connected it to the left and right banks. Only a 100 years
or so after the Romans went home, the original tribe who had
built their wooden fort on the mosquito infested island and
traded on the river in their dugout boats, had the last laugh.
They were called the *Parisii*, which actually means 'boatmen',
and it is their name which Paris enshrines, and their emblem,
an unsinkable boat, which is the badge of Paris to this day.

After the Romans had left, a wave of Barbarians threatened
Paris, but a local girl of the fifth century, Ste Geneviève,
persuaded the Parisians against flight or panic, saying that
their protection was assured by Heaven, and that the
destruction would take place further south, as indeed it did,
Attilla meeting defeat near Orléans. When the Franks laid
seige to Paris, reducing the population to near starvation, it
was Geneviève who organised the river traders to take their
boats by stealth through the marsh streams and channels that
they knew well, up to Champagne, and bring the boats back
loaded to the gunwales with supplies for the hungry town.

For ninety years Geneviève succoured her beleaguered
people whenever they needed it, against famine and sickness
and enemy attack, and managed a few run-of-the-mill miracles
as well; and when she died she was buried in a church specially
built by King Clovis, on the mound known thereafter as the
Montagne Ste Geneviève, where the Pantheon now stands.
Since she is the patroness of Paris, it would be comforting to
think that her bones were still in some mediaeval chapel here,
in the beautiful golden reliquary fashioned for her remains by
the Goldsmith-Bishop Saint Eloi, but this was melted down at
La Monnaie in 1793, during the Terror, and her bones were
sacrilegiously burned and the ashes thrown into the Seine.

Unlike the Rhône, the Gironde, and the Dordogne, the Seine
posed no problems of navigation to the ships that used it since
before the times of the Romans. They were light in weight and
shallow draughted. In the Middle Ages, the City grew
inordinately, and in stone, not wood, pillaging the quarries and
gravel pits nearby to build innumerable palaces and guildhalls
on the Right Bank, colleges and universities on the Left Bank,
close to the Montagne Ste Geneviève, and churches and
chapels everywhere.

Only now did the *mariniers* complain, and loudly, about the throwing of quantities of building rubbish into the river. The debris, they said, had raised the water level and unequally at that; it now formed a barrage between upstream and down of up to 1.70 metres. What is more, they complained, the bridges you are building have massive stone piers and low headroom which impede our progress, and all these mills and pumps associated with the building are making it difficult for us to ply our trade. The Seine, from being the easiest of rivers to navigate, had become, at Paris, a double dead end. The River Traders' *raison d'être* was to supply the city with everything it required, including building materials, roads being slow and hazardous where they existed at all. The River Trader's Guild was the most powerful and highly respected, the *mariniers'* voice was heard, and the privileges that they long held from the Kings and Lords in whose gift it was, were increased. In addition to the right of charging dues and tolls on the Seine, pilotage of the passage through Paris, which was now hazardous and required local knowledge, was provided by the *Marchands d'Eau*, the River Traders themselves. At a price, of course.

In the twelfth century, they installed themselves on the Right Bank and no doubt snickered as they watched any craft that dared to attempt the passage downstream without their expert and expensive aid wrap itself round the pillars of the Pont-au-Change. In the other direction, they provided ropes and a service to haul the boats against the current upstream. Chains across the Seine denoted the Péage, and the barges would have to wait till all dues were paid before the barrier would be lowered and the convoy allowed through.

Our progress however, was unimpeded by chains, though we were slowed down at one point by building works connected with a tunnel being built under the Seine. What would the *Marchands d'Eau* have thought of that, I wonder. Tolls and dues nowadays are paid to the VNF (the *Voies Navigables de France*) and are valid for all French waterways. Chains and barriers exist no more, except when the *mariniers*, no longer a powerful Guild with privileges, their *métier* in decline and their respected status gone, draw attention to the grievance by blocking the river or canal with their barges. If they choose a moment when a Minister is being treated to a boat tour it can be an effective protest.

A passage by water is a wonderful way to see the City, since once past the industrial outskirts and the railway yards the timeworn utilities of warehouse and factory give place to equally timeworn but superbly graceful architecture, palaces, churches, museums, and state buildings, set among parks on handsome quays.

We went between two monumental stations: the Gare de Lyon on our right and the Gare d'Austerlitz on our left. Most of the river banks are beautifully laid out, the splendid buildings complemented by gardens and parks, the quays are elegantly furnished with trees and lamps, and many of the thirty-three bridges are works of art.

Bill remarked that it was not his favourite city, but then he does not like cities. He feels that ten thousand inhabitants is the biggest number of people who can live in close proximity with any hope of remaining civilised. Laurel likes even smaller places, as a town that she can walk around has about four thousand inhabitants, but she has wishful thoughts about the art and culture and learning that is to be found in great cities. Bill asks why such things cannot be produced without the manure of decadence.

While debating these niceties we had passed with interest the entrance to the Arsenal, which is the Port de Plaisance of Paris, where barges such as *Hosanna* could berth if they wished to stay and visit the city. It is a narrow exit and is served by traffic lights. No one was coming or going, and the lights were in our favour.

We cannot explain what happened next, except to say that it was stupidity, carelessness, too strong a sense of history and a failure to consult the chart. We found ourselves at the Pont Sully, the bridge above the Ile St Louis. Bill failed to notice until it was almost too late that there were traffic lights on it, and they were clearly directed at barge traffic. These were not in our favour. They were uncompromisingly, unforgivingly, red. We had arrived rather suddenly at the one way system that carries you southwest of the Ile St Louis and northeast of the Ile de la Cité. It was absolutely *défendu* to proceed; we must wait for a green light, to allow traffic to come upstream.

We were fairly near to disaster as he put the engine into full astern, trying to stop us with a strong current carrying us down towards the bridge abutments, and the off-centre engine swinging the ship round so that we stood a good chance of straddling two abutments and being pinned there for ever. Laurel says she could hear the ghosts of old River Traders snickering. Then the stone embankment at the end of the Ile St Louis approached, much too close for comfort, the rocks that underpinned the stone were horribly visible under our stern. Gradually Bill won *Hosanna* round, extracting us with some skill from a predicament which he should have avoided in the first place.

When we had stemmed the current we made fast to the left bank, on an attractive parklike quay, now that we had time to look at it. Bill consulted the river guide, which we should have done at the start of the day's journey. He had failed to notice the alternative traffic direction round the Ile St Louis and the Ile de la Cité; twenty five minutes each way, with a twenty minute gap to wait for the longish channel to clear before the lights changed. We had no idea how long we still had to wait, but having moored we could recover our breath and have a cup of coffee.

It was the Quai St Bernard and the park behind it was the Jardin des Plantes, first laid out by Louis XIII. It is a Parisian combination of Kew and the Zoo. We noted the down-and-outs sleeping in the warm morning sun – no need for the Come-all-ye shelter under the bridges of Paris today. The toes of their shabby trainers pointed to the blue sky (the boot with emerging toes is an out-of-date image) and often a bottle was tenderly cradled in an armpit. Energetically amorous students from the ancient universities made interesting use of statues, since the benches were occupied by somnolent tramps. The students were obviously enjoying that post-exam end-of-term euphoria when no work need be done and the pleasures of the flesh can be thoroughly explored. Close by on the Montagne Ste Geneviève Peter Abelard, that handsome, charismatic twelfth century scholar, held his students spellbound with dialectics, and scandalised the monks with his delight in the pleasures of the flesh. The clergy were horrified not so much by Abelard making love to Héloise, one of his pupils, as by neither of them caring who knew about it.

In the end we did not have to wait the full forty minutes, pondering on the eventful history of Abelard and Héloise, and its links with the foundation of the university. The light changed to green. We had unkindly shut the cats below, fearing to lose them in some flower bed, or worse that they would leap in friendly fashion upon a sleeping *clochard*, with unforeseen consequences. So we were off once more without delay, under the Pont Sully, jinking to the right from the Bras de la Tournelle between the Ile St Louis and the Ile de la Cité, and passing Notre Dame, close and spectacular on our left. As we were going downstream we had to be content with the back view, obscured by trees. If you want to see the front of this masterpiece of Gothic building, and see it from the river, you must come upstream because of the one-way system, using the Bras de la Monnaie, which to this day has so strong a current that in times of flood it is closed to all traffic.

The shipshaped Ile de la Cité, which is anchored in the river like a huge liner with brows to both shores, is the oldest part of the City, though there are few traces of the Parisii who first settled there.

In a kilometre and a half we had passed from the Left Bank, site of ancient seats of learning often based on monasteries, and their heritors the universities, colleges and libraries of today, to the even more ancient mercantile area on the Right Bank. On our right the Hotel de Ville stands on what used to be called the Place de Grève, the Mediaeval centre of commerce. Here as early as the eleventh century the Guild of River Traders had bossed the shipping on the Seine. Anywhere along these quays when the Black Death ravaged Paris the innumerable dead were tossed into the river, the tossers calling on Ste Geneviève to help them, her reputation against the Plague being well established. Here, ironically, poor Geneviève's ashes were also tossed into the Seine during the Terror.

At the end of the Ile de la Cité we passed under the Pont Neuf, the New Bridge, which is nevertheless the oldest existing bridge of the thirty three, just as New College is the oldest in Oxford.

The buildings of the Louvre passed majestically to our right. In the gardens of the Tuileries mothers walked their small children in the shade of the trees while the older ones were at school for yet a few more days before the summer holidays began.

We passed the Place de la Concorde, where in 1793 the crowds cheered as the Guillotine lopped the powdered head of Marie Antionette on the twenty fifth day of Vendomiaire. We passed between the Palais de Chaillot (1937) on our right and the Eiffel tower (1889) on our left, and remembered that Gustave Eiffel was also the architect of the beautiful Pont-canal at Briare which we had crossed two weeks earlier.

Down through the heart of this busy city we sailed through a thousand years, with 20th century traffic roaring along either embankment and across the bridges above our heads, while on either side the quays were full of floating palaces of glass, the Bateaux-Mouches, loading their cargoes of tourists in preparation for the day's excursions. If we envied them at all, it was for the chance to go upstream in the Bras de la Monnaie. We could not afford the time to do a round trip.

Soon after this the historical elegance ended, and practicality took charge again: the Maison de Radio-France, Sports Halls, the Heliport, Electricité de France, until the river was flanked by moored barges and tanks and silos and marshalling yards again. The closed and disused Renault factory occupied every single square centimetre of the Ile Séguin, like a rusty hulk, sheets of metal descending down to the water's very edge, no grass, no strand, an island of red powdery steel and decaying concrete several storeys high, where ghosts of the carworkers, whose physical bodies are now resettled in the green country-side, gazed back from one of France's worst urban eyesores at a beautiful city through broken panes of sooty glass. We were through the heart of Paris and it was still only half past ten in the morning.

We did seventy kilometres that day, with the Seine flowing fast under us, and only three locks to pass.

Finally we made fast to the town quay at Conflans-St-

Honorine, close to the fire-boat, where it said: PUSHER-TUGS ONLY. There was plenty of room, but we waited, ready to move out if a determined PUSHER appeared, but none did. So we set off ashore. 'My hand is itching,' said Laurel. 'I think it's time the stitches came out.' We checked the log and it was indeed a week since the injury. The doctor who had done the original tailoring job had foreseen no problem. Any *pharmacien* would do it, he said airily. Simple. We entered the nearest chemist's. The *pharmacien* at Conflans gave an elegant shudder and declined positively (or should that be negatively?) to have anything to do with it. Considering that in some of the remoter parts of France pharmacists have only recently given up enthusiastic leeching, and we mean with real leeches, we were surprised. Laurel hushed Bill's nascent comment about the lady's lack of spirit. 'You must go the *clinique*,' said the chemist, firmly. We were probably too close to Paris. We doubt if she had ever tangled with leeches.

The first *clinique* we found turned out to be an orthodontist who would take out teeth, but not stitches. He sent us to another *clinique*, down the quay. This one was an ophthalmologist. He could remove foreign bodies from eyes, but not stitches from hands. 'Didn't they teach you how?' Bill enquired testily before Laurel could control him. The doctor showed us out with icy rapidity.

It is becoming more and more difficult in the so-called advanced countries to find a medical practitioner whose knowledge encompasses the entire body. You have a finger problem, so you find a finger specialist, BUT he is an *index* finger specialist and your problem is with the *little* finger. Try again your second attempt produces a doctor who is a little finger specialist BUT only on the *right* hand. Your problem is the *left*. Sorry. It is possible to go on with this little saga almost indefinitely.

It was extremely hot and Laurel's walking distance had been more than accomplished. At such times, she tends to sit down firmly, like Queen Victoria, and request refreshment. Since *Hosanna* was close by we returned on board. Both of us have done the Ship Captain's medical course. Both of us can, for instance, give injections and insert stitches in wounds. Theoretically, that is, meaning that we know how, but so far we have only practised on oranges, or on lumps of polyurethane foam under supervision. It is a little different confronted with warm pulsating flesh.

Nevertheless we decided that together we would do what the combined medical resources of France were evidently incapable of doing that evening. We gave ourselves half an hour's rest, then Bill used the little scissors on his Swiss army knife to snip the stitches, and Laurel's jewellery pliers to extract them. After sterilizing the requisites liberally in medicinal alcohol, we need hardly add. We then took a glass of internal antiseptic (brandy and ginger with ice) in case we'd swallowed any germs, while Laurel contemplated the little holes on the back of her hand.

'I'll do,' she said.

· 10 ·

CASUALTY IN THE CANALS

In which we meet a spare-parts courier – the barge museum – the chapel in a barge – Friends' corner – and we do not see eye to eye with a doctor

We badly needed a pause at Conflans-Ste-Honorine. Bill was still physically below par, though the hay fever season seemed over (or perhaps we were now nearer the potato fields of the North) and his bronchial infection had cleared up. Perhaps St Aventin (Colds and Fevers) had had a hand in this. Nevertheless it had left him tiring easily and with few reserves of good temper to cope with our often infirmities. (Our family has always thoroughly agreed with the advice contained in St Paul's Epistle to Timothy: 'Use a little wine for thy stomach's sake and thine often infirmities'.) The Saint to cope with long hours and short temper (St Gerasimos, Minor Mental Disorders) was incontrovertibly Greek, and territorial, and not likely to displace himself for our benefit.

On our arrival the day before, Laurel had requested a young bystander if he would be so *gentil* as to take a mooring rope. 'Of course,' he said, 'But you don't have to speak French.' This young Englishman with the unusual name of Armatie was of Ghanaian origin, but in comportment, diction and manner was thoroughly Anglo-Saxon. He led an interesting life and was interested in ours. Being in the entertainment business, he had periods when he was resting and needed occasionally to enhance his earnings. He would then spend a few days helping the Ford Motor Company to manage their Just-in-time part-procurement programme.

Ford concentrate the manufacture of components for their cars at several different sites, some of them at wholly-owned subsidiary companies and some at outside contractors. In times past they used to maintain a large stock of parts at Dagenham to avoid problems of strikes, transport and general break-downs. They feel nowadays that the enormous cost of maintaining this stock is no longer justified with the improvements in transport and industrial relations. They organise the deliveries of these parts to arrive only as they are needed, just in time.

Inevitably things go wrong, and then it pays them to hire a reliable courier to make an express journey to bring over enough of the particular part to keep the production lines going. It all sounds very chancy to us, but we presume that Ford have costed it carefully, since stopping a production line is clearly a dramatic event.

Armatie had the courier job of driving over on the ferry, picking up a quantity of left-handed widgets from a factory near Paris, and rushing them over to Dagenham. He would be here at the same time tomorrow, and if we didn't move on, we'd see him again, he said, he always lunched here on the riverside.

It was a fine warm day and we relaxed in our verandah, that part of the boat abaft the wheelhouse where we can sit as in a garden (indeed it is where we grow our parsley) and enjoy the air, the view, and indulge in the continental pastime of commenting on the dress, habits, and deportment of passers-by. Conversely the passers-by can and do comment on us. When we felt too lazy even to make our own mid-morning cup of coffee, we walked the ten or so metres over to the quayside café, and even had a sticky cake to go with it. Bill was making a great effort to behave himself, Laurel was relieved after the trauma of a surgical operation performed by an unqualified surgeon (it was healing beautifully, and why shouldn't it?).

Armatie joined us. Since we had a son learning script writing, we had a lot to talk about until he had to leave to catch his ferry.

After lunch we treated ourselves to a long promised visit to la Musée de la Batellerie (the Inland Waterways Museum), high up on the hill overlooking the town, with a wonderful view over the confluence after which the town is named: that of the rivers Seine and Oise. This is a most interesting and well ordered museum. We had a talk with the curator, a learned and obviously dedicated man who was about to retire. We discussed the alterations which had been made to the Canal de la Somme by the British Royal Engineers in order to supply the enormous army in the infamously mis-managed Battle of the Somme in 1916. There is no documentation on this in France; presumably it was all done in a hurry with no consultation, which is not surprising given the circumstances. The Museum would much appreciate any information, especially pictures, of the canal in use during this battle.

We admired the drawings and models and artefacts all the more since we own a barge ourselves, albeit a seagoing one, which the French do not understand at all. Their *péniches* (barges) are forbidden to leave the canals, and therefore French yachtsmen are astonished when they meet *Hosanna* in Corsica or Sicily or the Greek Islands, where we have obviously arrived by sea.

'Have you the right to do this?' they tend to ask us, dubiously. 'We, the English and the Dutch, have the right,' we crow. 'French *péniches* do not.' We try to imply without actually saying so that no one in their right mind would *want* to go to sea in a *péniche*, whereas the English and the Dutch build strong and seaworthy barges that will cope with coastal and offshore work as well as inland waters. They have even crossed the Atlantic. In our wilder moments, we dream of going Transatlantic again ourselves. The thought comes when the canals are throwing their worst at us, in the way of surly lock-keepers, delays, bad moorings, automatic devices that refuse to trigger (still to come) and *chômages* (stoppages for canal maintenance: we did not encounter one of these latter on the whole journey, mercifully.)

We paused on the grassy terraces of the Museum to gaze at the confluence of the two rivers spread out awesomely below us. We could trace tomorrow's journey up the river Oise and out of sight, a view seldom gifted to us, travelling at sea level as we do. Then we descended the hill and walked further along

114

the quayside where is moored the Chapel-barge *Je Sers* (I serve). We managed adroitly to avoid an excited party of schoolchildren, who were making a great noise about being shown round, and went on board with leisure to make a calm examination. In the foyer were large noticeboards acquainting bargees with news, professional, religious and social from all over their special world: *Piques-niques*, Marriages, Christenings, Pilgrimages and *Pardons*. This chapel, once a coal barge, has since 1937 served the *Batellerie* (the barge folk) both as a parish church and source of social welfare. There is a comfortable hall for social events, a large and elegant chapel with stained glass windows, statues of the saints beloved of bargees, such as St Nicholas, St Roch, Ste Rita, not forgetting Ste Honorine herself, and behind the altar hung two anchors of the kind that we East Anglians call rond-hooks.

We learnt that Ste Honorine, virgin and martyr, who gives her name to Conflans, is the Patron Saint of Bateliers. She is especially appealed to by the barge wives for a safe childbirth. Tradition tells that she was a Gallo-Roman from Graville near Harfleur, martyred in the fourth century when she refused to abjure her faith before the Roman proconsul. Her martyrdom, judging by the only picture we have seen, was Gilbertian: 'something lingering, with boiling oil in it, I fancy,' since she is shown in a cauldron surrounded by leaping flames. Her body was then thrown into the Seine at Tancarville, carried by the waves to her home town, Graville, where Christians recovered her and placed her in a tomb. Here she rested quietly, doing no harm to anyone, for the next four hundred years. The coming of the Norman invaders to the coast threw everything awry.

The monks in charge of the relics decided that translation (we would nowadays call it evacuation) was necessary, and in those days of non-existent roads, how would they do this but by boat? In 876 Ste Honorine's bones journeyed up the Seine to the confluence of the two rivers, probably loaded tenderly into a barge. At Conflans the bones were placed in the Sanctuary of Notre Dame, which, 200 years later, burned down. The bones, a little calcined, were saved. A new church was ready to receive them in 1087 and a festival of Translation was organised, under the command of one Anselm, Abbot of

Bec in Normandy, later Archbishop of Canterbury, and in time himself promoted to Saint.

Pilgrims hearing of this, naturally flocked to the confluence, and began to cross the Seine to join in the fun. Like all tourists en masse, and en fête, they were giggling too much to pay heed to safety regulations, and too many of them crowded into a boat which rapidly began to sink. They gave despairing tongue. They shruck, as we say in Norfolk, appealing to the monks on the other side for aid. Anselm seized the skull of Ste Honorine and with it made the sign of the cross. The boat righted itself and came across safely with all its passengers.

Thenceforth Ste Honorine was adopted as the local patronne of the Batellerie. We stress local, since as we already indicated there is quite a choice of Saints for *mariniers* or *bateliers* (both words mean those who gain their living on river boats). Except for St Nicholas, who is invoked everywhere by deep sea sailors and rivermen alike, their tutelage tends to be regional and specific, such as: St Roch of St Satur and the Loire, (Plague and dog bites), St Gilles of the Rhône (Tempest) and St Clement, Loire (Drowning). We have mentioned Ste Rita for Desperate Causes and the Impossible (her territory is Northern France and into Belgium) and those numerous and widespread Saints in charge of Dangerous Passages.

The Museum on its hill and the Chapel *Je Sers* moored in the Seine made sense of all this. The life of the *marinier* and his family was always encompassed by hardship if not downright danger. Now unfair road and rail competition threaten both his livelihood and his very way of life. One barge carries 40 lorry loads, and does it quietly, unpollutingly, and without killing anyone, yet the trade declines, and the powers that be will not see sense. The *batelier* cannot live without hope. The Saints of his *métier*, with their own territories and special areas of concern that are his too, give him that hope.

To end our day off we decided to dine at the Restaurant Confluence de l'Oise, quite a little way from our boat. It had been a hot and tiring day, but a shower revived us like thirsty flowers, and we found the motivation to walk there gently. This restaurant proudly boasted a star from the very strict Michelin inspectors, and we had not come across many of those.

The restaurant was quite full, but we secured a good table out of doors and enjoyed our evening. We stayed late savouring the sunset over the water, and waiting for the heat to soak away a little. When it was time to go we asked if the management would call a taxi for us. The proprietor of this large establishment had just knocked off. She and her son had come out front to say goodnight to patrons, and to enjoy a drink and a smoke. 'My son is going back to town,' she said. 'He will drive you.' Such a pleasant courtesy should not go unsung. We hope a French family touring in England would enjoy similar treatment. Fortunately we know of just such an incident. Generosity and courtesy are not dead, on either side of the Channel.

The following morning broke cloudy and blowy, and we left the Seine to go up the river Oise. It is a winding river and it is used by some very substantial barges which make the problem worse by navigating in tandem, thus requiring very large turning circles. When these are coming downstream in times of spate, and are turning without brakes in turbulent water to pass under narrow arches of ancient bridges over the river, then small boats watch out: a collision in these circumstances would not just be an uncomfortable bump. No wonder the footbridge at Conflans has a statue of St Nicholas (Tempests and Drowning) niched on it, Heaven protect us all.

We had an uneventful passage. The river was fairly wide and deep, and Laurel could be trusted with the wheel again, freeing Bill for other duties. We had some fun with the name of the river, on the lines of 'This wuz the Oise, wuz it?' 'Yes, it wuz.' We did a (for us) fast run of seventy kilometres and only four locks, and in the evening made fast to a broken-down quay at St Maxence. Laurel did not feel like cooking, she had had a hard day's driving, and so we went out in search of a meal.

We noted the position of the elegant restaurant, but it being still too early to dine, went for a drink at the little riverside café, Le Coin des Amis (The Friends' Corner). This turned out to be full of *bateliers*. The proprietor and his wife had retired from their barge life, and their children were away somewhere carrying a cargo of animal feed. When they knew that we were from a barge, moored close by, everyone present welcomed us with great warmth. We had common cause, and the conversation was lively and good-humoured, ranging widely over sport, politics (those dreadful people in Brussels: does anyone except their own mothers love them?), the decrepitude of the canals and the state of trade. The establishment served simple food; better a dinner of herbs where love is, we said to ourselves, and forgot the stalled ox at the elegant restaurant. We ate in the *Coin* among friends.

As we left the river the next day and entered the Canal du Nord we no longer experienced any problems of boat handling with our off-centre screw. We were now in the North, and the canal was heading towards the heavy industry of Lille and the Belgian border. It was built for big barges and was wider and deeper than the canals of the *Centre* and we were able to get along with little difficulty. We were going into desolate country, some of it hilly, and we were sometimes not sure if a lock would take us up or down. Towns and villages became less frequent. Moorings were harder to find, and we had to continue until the locks closed for the night at 1930 and then made fast to the lock quay. It was the last day of June. Laurel produced an excellent supper of a fish stew with monkfish tails and mussels.

The tunnels on this canal are well maintained and easy to negotiate. We had been dreading the prospect of tunnels again, and had chosen this route partly because they would be shorter than those on the alternative. We passed the first on the following day without delays or problems, and then needing fresh provisions again stopped for the night at a silo quay close to the village of Moislains. The guide book said that water was available at this quay. It lied. The village too, was sparsely served by commerce. Everything seemed closed, including the café. It had a run-down air.

At the first lock after the second tunnel we got into a queue of barges and had to wait two hours for our turn. The barge crews, also delayed, were all a bit bad-tempered, and they handled their boats with less than the usual consideration for others; there was shouting and some display of gallic temperament, though not directed at us. Laurel stood to one side of the quay as one impatient barge swept past, much too fast, jerking our mooring rope tight and parting it. She was standing too close to the bollard, and the tail end of the 25 mm diameter, whip-cracking rope caught her across the shin. A swelling like an orange came up instantly, but was reduced by sitting for an hour with an ice-pack on it. We did not on this occasion have to resort to a pack of frozen peas, as we have done in the past. Nothing wrong with that, it works, and you can eat your cataplasm for supper.

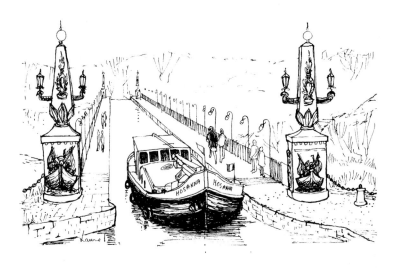

It came to us that we were suffering physically more than usual on this voyage. Which Saint was in charge? Whom to appeal to? Probably Charlemagne (Preserver from Accidents). At least we did not need St Fiacre (Haemorrhoids). Probably the strain was telling and we no longer had the reactions and alertness that are customary to us. Perhaps we were also continuing our run of bad luck. There was no profit in telling Laurel she should not have stood where she did. She knew that perfectly well. She told Bill as much. But it still hurt like hell.

At Marquion there was a good quay near the village street. We stopped and talked to a French Yachtie, Bernard, who was doing some work on his boat, and Laurel having even less aptitude for walking than usual, Bill went to do the shopping.

Laurel did the cooking, *quenelles de perche* with a lobster sauce, salads and patisserie.

It was at this point, already three weeks late getting to England, but at last within striking distance of Calais, that Bill had more trouble with his eyes, and we once again became involved with French medicine. This time the result was very different from the last.

At Aigues-Mortes some two years previously, Bill had experienced on Good Friday some bright flashes in his left eye. He was not over-concerned until next morning when the vision in that eye had gone cloudy. Consulting our medical guides, we found unequivocal advice to seek expert help without any delay.

In France if one has an eye problem one contacts directly an ophthalmic surgeon. One does not have to go to a GP to be told 'You have an eye problem; now you must see an ophthalmologist (if there is still any point in doing so by the time I have arranged your appointment)'. We looked in the yellow pages, and wonder of wonders, there was an 'ophthalmo' in the nearby village of Vauvert, 6000 inhabitants. Told by phone to come without delay, Bill was examined, a tear in the retina diagnosed by Dr. Romano, who then drove us in the car to the clinic in the departmental capital. Although it was now noon on Easter Saturday, within a few minutes of arrival Bill was given a local anesthetic and some 300 laser 'stitches' in the retina of his eye. The doctor drove us back again. We gave him a eurocheque for about £120, that is some £85 for the operation, and the rest for some drugs that had been prescribed.

A few days later, Laurel had taken the receipt to the SECU (the bureau who deal with medical payments) and in a surprisingly short time we received a giro cheque for most of what we had paid the doctor. It was all very efficient and satisfactory, and we were grateful to young Dr Romano.

The clouds in the eye did not clear as quickly as Dr Romano had predicted, and being conscious that the gentleman was young and provincial, Bill had decided to consult the retinal clinic at St Thomas' in London a few weeks later, where he was already an occasional patient. They inspected the left eye closely, and endorsed the young doctor's work as first class with the equipment he would have had available. Being a teaching hospital at the leading edge, they had the means of tidying up the inaccessible ends of the torn retina; all went well, and we were now grateful to the experts of both countries.

Now the same thing seemed to have happened in the other eye, and again on a Saturday. This time we ended up in the casualty department of the *hôpital conventionnée* at the city nearby. It was in full Saturday night swing, treating drunks, assault victims, injured workers, overdoses and accidents. It was bedlam. A crowd of travellers had accompanied their wounded relative, and were noisily giving everyone a hard time. We had a very long uncomfortable wait. It was one in the morning before Bill was seen by a very young casualty doctor, who immediately called the duty ophthalmologist, whom we shall call Dr Toubib. The latter made an examination and then came the shock.

This is a serious matter, we were told. The retina is detached and badly torn. You will come into hospital immediately, spend two or three days in hospital on your back to prepare for an operation under general anesthetic, which will be Wednesday or Thursday, and two days in hospital to recover.

A week. And you nearly always come out of hospital with more bugs than you went in with. Resistant ones, too.

Hang on, we said. If Bill has the capacity to be grateful to doctors who have done him well, he is also cautious by nature. Having experienced the whole thing once before, he had some idea of how things should go. 'I can still see out of that eye,' he said. 'With a detached retina that surprises me very much,' said the Doctor, disbelieving. Bill declined the offer to be admitted straightaway, to everyone's astonishment but Laurel's (they had a trolley all ready to put him on), but took a number to call, just in case. We wanted to go back to our boat and think, we said. If you would prefer the operation in England we could arrange your transport by special ambulance, said Dr Toubib quickly; special because you must stay on your back and not be jolted. We repeated our need for time to think. Since no operation was envisaged till the next Wednesday, the doctor could not argue that it was urgent, and

Bill could as well lie on his back in the boat as in hospital. Laurel did not say that to keep Bill on his back in any circumstances would require nothing less than knockout drops. Nor did we say that we also wanted a second opinion. One thing both Dr Romano and St Thomas's had stressed was that speed in retina cases was desirable.

The next morning, Sunday, Bill rang the duty ophthalmologist at St Thomas' and sought his advice, describing his symptoms. 'We can probably do it with a local anesthetic tomorrow morning. Nothing you tell me suggests that you should not travel. Can you get here?' he was asked. Any way but barge, England was so close. Why not? Bernard was happy to feed our cats for a day or so, and keep an eye on *Hosanna*.

That very afternoon we crossed the channel by ferry, and Bill duly presented himself at the retinal clinic on Monday morning. He had a poor start because they had lost his papers, but the surgeon was not put out. A quick but very thorough examination, then another opinion from a more senior colleague.

'This is a perfectly simple tear in the retina, not nearly as serious as your previous one, and there is no detachment. We will laser it up straightaway. General anesthetic? Certainly not.' It was done in no time. 'How had Dr Toubib come to make his diagnosis?' asked Bill. 'We can but conjecture,' said the British Professor tactfully, and would say no more.

We, however, continued to ask ourselves: why? No competent opthalmologue could have made such a mistake. Ophthalmology in France is generally as well advanced as in England (they claim it to be more so), their universities are as competent, their teaching as good.

A clue comes, perhaps, from the prosecution and sentencing of a surgeon in Toulouse who had been found guilty of carrying out operations that were completely unnecessary. At least he was caught out and punished. His crime is apparently not that uncommon.

As far as Dr Toubib knew, we were ordinary English tourists on a short visit, covered by the usual travel insurance with a get-you-home clause. This would almost certainly cover the fees for a serious in-patient operation of the kind he was proposing, or if not, the expense of the ambulance trip back to England if its necessity were medically certified. The cost of the operation would have been considerable. The cost of the repatriation also. To whom would these monies have gone? Who might or might not have got a cut?

We cannot say, and can only speculate. If it had not already happened to Bill's other eye, we would have done as Dr Toubib wished, in great distress and panic, lost a whole week, and gained who knows what nokosogenic ills. We do not have holiday insurance. We try to steer clear of hospitals.

As it was, we were back on board, all shipshape and with an excellent prognosis, by Tuesday lunchtime. We settled for having come out of the event in good order, but thought we would tell the story. But for this one incident, our experience of French medicine has engendered our deepest respect. Now, we believe we have also seen the flip side.

After thanking Bernard for looking after the cats (presenting him with the requested tin of Golden Syrup), we continued the voyage.

· 11 ·

CALOO CALAIS! OH FRABJOUS DAY!

In which we net a pigeon but miss 'The Swan' – make a
diversion – suffer automatic delay – see the sea – the
sails are set once more

Alone in Guinchy lock, we thought the exit gates had stuck,
we were in there so long. At all events the young *éclusier*
was looking anxiously down into the lock. We went to have a
look. There was a pigeon in the water. 'I think it is hurt,' said
the *éclusier*. 'If it cannot fly, it will be killed when I open the
gates.'

'We have a net,' we said, and went to get it. The young man
was then able to reach the pigeon, which he lifted with extreme
gentleness and cradled in his bosom. It seemed perfectly
trusting. 'See,' he said 'He has been shot. I will remove the
balle from the wing, and he will heal.' We commended his
compassion. 'Oh, it is a passion with me,' he said. 'I have
many *pigeons voyageurs* at home. Here is the ring on the foot
to tell me who is the owner. This is a Belgian pigeon. I shall
send him back when he is well.' He laid it tenderly on his desk,
and set about opening the lock gates.

If only all our delays had been so justified.

We decided on a slight diversion to St Omer. It would not
take us long, we thought. There is an excellent restaurant in St
Omer called Le Cygne where we had often eaten very well. We
were now so close to Calais that we felt moderate celebration
was in order. We might not get another chance.

When the canal was enlarged and modernised in the sixties,
it was felt impossible to alter that part which passed through
the old town of St Omer, with houses close to the edge of

either bank, and with its two ancient locks. So a bypass was built through the marshes with only one deep lock. The town had insisted on its existing canal remaining open, so The Navigation, as the canal authority is known, closed the lock and canal below the town, thus turning St Omer into the terminus of a branch canal approached by its southern lock and an old fashioned swing bridge. To navigate up to St Omer one must call ahead so that *pontiers* and *éclusiers* can be on duty to let you through.

We called ahead. Unfortunately the entrance to the side canal was blocked by *péniches* awaiting cargoes. A little shuffling, a difficult left-hand turn (we must have been mad to attempt this), and we were through the bridge without mishap, and up the narrow, old, shallow canal. After the lock we had problems. There had been the usual thunderstorm the previous evening, and it had poured water into the catchment area of the stream that debouched into the canal just below the lock. This rain had turned the little stream into a torrent and several tons of good French topsoil had washed down into the canal. We found it. And we stuck on it. We offered it back to the French. Please redistribute it over your fields, we pleaded. The head office of the Navigation was almost within shouting distance, so they were aware of our predicament, and engaged to raise the level. It would take a little time, they said.

It took a couple of hours. We unstuck thankfully and moored to the quay in St Omer. The delay had made us extra-ready for a good dinner, and we took ourselves to the town centre only to find that Le Cygne had changed its closing day and was shut. We sat in a café to compose the evil thoughts that were passing through our frustrated minds. Just who was ordering events so that we could not get even the simplest enjoyable experiences in good order? St Omer was clearly not a Batelier's Saint. On the other hand he had spent a good deal of his life sightless, so was presumably sympathetic to our eye problems.

There are other restaurants in St Omer, not in the same class as Le Cygne, but one of them would do. Walking to look for it, we passed a plumber's van belonging to one Patrick Pottie, Sanitaire, and shortly after saw a For Sale sign placed by a *notaire* with the entrancing name of Maitre Cocqenpot. Best of all was a notice at the moat which ran close to the ruins of the Abbaye of St Bertin (colleague of St Omer) which warned us:

PRELEVEMENT DE VERS DE VASE INTERDIT

We were not in a mood to dig mudworms, especially since it had been forbidden. These things and our meal, if not death-lessly memorable, cheered us up, for we are not naturally gloomy people. Restored to good spirits by food and a little juvenile laughter, we returned to our boat, had ourselves a good tot and slept well.

In the morning we found someone had stolen our alumini-um ladder.

To avoid running aground on leaving we had adverted the required officials, and though we stuck again, this time they were ready. Sluices were closed, and gradually the water level rose until we were able to float into the lock and escape. We thanked the good folk of La Navigation (now officially called VNF) and took our leave. We hoped to be in Calais that night. The big canal is easy, there was only one lock to pass. But the gods had not finished with us yet.

When we arrived at the Ecluse Hennuin we discovered it was an automatic lock. We were required to pull levers, twist rods, and wait for sirens to go, lights to flash, and things to happen. They did not happen. There is nothing more upsetting to the human soul than an automatic thingummy that does not automate. Laurel could see Bill's wrath reaching danger level as he toured the deserted surroundings looking for help. Surroundings in Flanders tend to be mile wide beet fields and a deserted silo. Help there was none. There was a button inviting *mariniers* in difficulty to press it. Bill did. He came close to assaulting it, he abused it roundly in French and English using nautical language that eased his troubled mind. No comforting little voice came over the tantalising loudspeaker near the button. Worse, no one was answering on VHF.

We decided to walk to the hamlet a few hundred metres down the canal and round the corner (a left-hand one to be sure). Surely there would be someone who could help. There would surely be a telephone on which we could call President

Mitterand (portrayed on the *Bébète Show*, the French version of *Spitting Image*, as the frog Kermit-erand) to press the case of two frustrated English allies stuck on his beastly canal. Perhaps he would have merely added a W to the word 'allies'.

We discovered in the hamlet that workmen were repairing the lift bridge over the canal. Pile drivers were hammering in piles where the bridge would normally be. We telephoned Authority. This was going on every day, the channel being cleared for navigation at 1700. Since one could not pass the

Lauwel.

bridge during the day, what was the point of opening the lock? The logic was French and impeccable. Had we not, asked Authority, been informed?

No we b*****y had not. We had passed through an *Ecluse de Controle* not long before where we had presented our papers and had a discussion with the *éclusier*. We had told him where we were bound. He had not mentioned any closures, or repairs, indeed he had wished us bon voyage, and told us we should have no problems all the way to Calais. Ah! but *monsieur, that écluse* is in the next section, he does not come under this office. Saperlipopette! Perhaps if Bill had not been speaking to the official on the phone he would have strangled him. Instead, he hung up. The lady at the café hearing of our difficulties, rang her friend the *pontier*. Her friend would come on her mobylette at 1700 and let us through both the lock and bridge. When dealing with government officials in any land it is never a question of what the rules are. It is a question of who you know.

The lady arrived at 1700 on the dot and passed us through the lock, together with a waiting commercial barge who also had not heard about the bridge repairs. We had hoped for some diverting gallic reaction but he had just shrugged and gone below for a sleep. Disappointing. The lesson is that the *mariniers* are inured to the inefficiencies of the people who run the canals.

Our inability to pass the lock and bridge at Hennuin till so late in the day left us with a longish run before Calais, but with the several lift or swing bridges ahead all automatic, we hoped to make it that night even though we envisaged a late arrival. We had reckoned without La Navigation's trump card. They switched off the automatic bridges at 1900, when we were still a bridge too far from Calais. OK, President Mitterand, you won this time, but we haven't had Waterloo yet.

The last bridge, at Coulogne, sat there like a sulky child. There was no quay, and no bitts to make fast to. Bill improvised a mooring to parts of the bridge and a sign that said AMARRAGE INTERDIT (No mooring), and he scrambled ashore to see what was what. He needed a beer. Five yards away from us was a *frites* stall, selling chips with various sausages of an improbable pink, doubtful hamburgers, and unimaginable and indescribable lumps of something that would be deep-fried on request. The stall was surrounded by young teenagers drinking coca cola and indulging in mild but noisily irritating horse-play.

Bill crossed the road to a café-restaurant; it was closed. Over the bridge was another rather scruffier bar where he got a beer. After his immediate thirst was assuaged and while waiting for his glass to be re-filled he contemplated a remarkable collection of military headgear, French, British and German caps, helmets, Képis, topees, pickelhaube, and so on, ranged across the wall. The café was also the centre of the pigeon-fanciers club. Bill calmed down chatting to the friendly local customers of the bar about their activities, telling them the story of the pigeon in the lock at Guinchy. Never judge a bar by a forbidding or scruffy exterior. The people inside are often neither.

We were underway early next day and not only arrived at Calais, but actually passed through the sea-lock, crossed the outer harbour and locked into the Bassin Ouest by mid morning. We were high as kites, as it was a major waypoint. We had accomplished 1424 kilometres since entering the Canals at the Mediterranean end, and 208 locks. Our inability to do left-hand turns with any ease had at one time suggested that we could end up in Leningrad rather than Calais. All we had to do now was get the masts up and make the hundred mile or so sea crossing to Great Yarmouth. All we had to do.

While Laurel went to telephone our arrival to anyone who would be interested, and then do some much needed shopping, Bill raised sheerlegs on the foredeck and re-stepped our foremast, not a light undertaking on his own. Then up went the mizzenmast, and that was enough for the day. We went to celebrate with a good dinner at Le Channel Restaurant which is Calais' best in our view.

It was blowing up a bit the next day, 7 July, but with the help of Mark, of the boat *Constellation*, who had been our companion for the last few automatic locks and bridges (they had pressed the buttons for us if it was a left handed approach), we had the mainmast in place and the radar dome (the most awkward lift of all) remounted on the wheelhouse roof. There were still a few things to do, but everything started to fall into place. Gwen and Valerie, Australian literary buffs, arrived from Le Crotoy as arranged to have a long and loquacious lunch and take our two cats to their Bed and Breakfast establishment; the British quarantine laws forbade us to bring them to England. Our son was coming to help with the sea crossing to Great Yarmouth. We felt we might even get there.

Laurel occupied herself with putting the breakables away and storing ship. She found a friendly taxi-driver who took her up to the *hypermarché* and waited without overcharging. Bill secured the ship for sea, which is quite a different requirement to that necessary for navigation in canals. He also bought wine and beer; it was our hope to repay much hospitality in England while we were there, so that was a substantial need, and we stocked up royally. We have over the years come to enjoy our wine, and enough bottles for two or more months came to quite a weight.

It is an interesting fact that while cheap wines are much less expensive in France than in England, the opposite applies to expensive wines of quality. Though obviously the first cost of high class wines to the English retailer is more than to his French counterpart, he sells on for less. This says a lot for the efficiency of the English retailer *vis-à-vis* his continental rival.

When we had time, we watched with pleasure the twice daily opening of the sealock, an hour each side of high water, and noted the maritime comings and goings. Now the summer season had really begun, there were sometimes forty or so yachts entering and leaving the Bassin, and they came and went in waves with the opening of the bridge.

Our son and his girl-friend Claire joined us in the evening to help us on the sea passage to Great Yarmouth. It looked as if we would have the right weather to leave the next day, and the tides would be on our side most of the way. We had dreaded being held up by bad weather. You don't go to sea in a barge without a reasonable forecast, and Laurel, as Met Officer, had been monitoring the weather for several days. For today, Thames and Dover: Variable three becoming South three to four, weather fair, visibility moderate becoming good. What more could we want? Accuracy, actually.

We left at about noon. Our off-centre screw had one more nasty trick to play. Traffic in Calais harbour is very intense and it is firmly radio-controlled by highly skilled Port Officers. Whoever is on duty balances the different needs of the big ferries ruled by timetables, large merchant ships locking in or out of the *bassins*, fishing boats, yachts with inexperienced skippers, and on this occasion a dredger working in the outer harbour. Normally it is all very efficient, but this Saturday 9th July things did not work out so well.

The Port Officer is bound by the unchanging ferry time-tables on one hand, and by the fact that access through the sealock to the *bassins* depends strictly on the height of the tide at any time, which changes day by day. Somehow today's duty man seemed to be losing the battle to balance all these things with the unstoppable clock and the unusually large number of yachts, let alone ferries, on this fine weekend morning in high season.

We had left the quay to try to hold our position ready to pass the lock. The amber stand-by lights were on, but the bridge did not open. Dozens of small yachts were careering about the basin like mullet round the sewer exit. The wind, while not dangerous, was strong enough to be troublesome from an awkward direction across the narrow basin. Unable to turn short because of our screw we were soon in difficulty, and drifted alongside our benefactor, *Constellation*. She is quite a small wooden boat and there was some concern that, though the impact had been gentle and fendered, the considerable weight of *Hosanna* could have caused some damage. Later we were reassured.

Bill called the Port Officer to ask how much further delay there would be before the *bassin* bridge opened, no doubt adding to his problems by doing so, but it had the desired effect, the green light came on, the bridge opened and about three dozen yachts of all sizes shot out into a small outer harbour already encumbered by a dozen or two yachts waiting to enter the basin, and the dredger. As soon as we left the basin the red lights at the signal station went on indicating that nobody was allowed to leave the harbour. On VHF we could hear the port officer talking to the huge cross channel ferries approaching outside, and requesting yachts to allow the *Côte d'Azur* to leave. Suddenly the lights went green-white-green. Like the start of the Grand National, dozens of yachts went full ahead and streamed for the pierheads.

We were in the van, largely because we could not maintain our position while stopped, could not turn, and had been creeping slowly ahead. As we neared the piers we saw two large ferries approaching; at the same time the leading ferry saw the fleet of small boats spread right across the fairway, which they were quite entitled to do with the signal on 'Go ahead'. He must have been horrified. It was too late for the ferry to put his engines astern and stop. For a moment Bill's heart was in his mouth, then he smiled as he saw the ferry start a 360° turn, sharp round to seaward, a brilliant manoeuvre in the limited space available. Ship-handling was Bill's *metier;* he knows a good seaman when he sees one.

The Port Officer on radio asked all the yachts to clear the fairway. Most, presumably heading westwards from the harbour mouth were over to the west side of the fairway, and huddled behind the west pier. As our plan was to head out northwards from Calais across the sand banks (it was high tide) we were thus coming out close to the eastern pierhead. We heard the *Pride of Bruges*, the second of the two ferries (the first was still only halfway through his turn), ask the Port Officer 'Do you know where the barge is heading?' Bill responded at once, and asked him which berth he was heading for, offering to keep clear in whichever way the ferry wished. We were thanked with what sounded like relief, the ferry was heading for No 2 berth; would we keep close to the eastern pier, please.

This we did. Actually we kept a little too close to the pier for comfort, under-estimating the strength of the tide sweeping across the entrance, which was running rather faster than our full speed, but Bill saw the problem in time, and our stern cleared the rocks by about ten metres, which is not very much in this context, but we did it. We are well aware of the difficulties big ships have manoeuvring in restricted space encumbered with dozens of little yachts. Suddenly we were offshore and leaving the Sandettie buoy to port, and we had space and air and lots of sky, and the sea, for the first time since the Mediterranean two months ago, just moving gently under our three keels. We were on our way north to Great Yarmouth and we felt wonderful.

· 12 ·

HOSANNA IN A HURRY

In which we cross the North Sea – into fog – delays on
land – obsequies for the monster – the final blow

Most people assume that the sea is more frightening,
more dangerous, and altogether much harder work
than the canals. Of course the sea in a bad mood is all of these
things, but we try to watch the weather and do our sea
passages when it is good tempered. Under these circumstances
being at sea is considerably less tiring than rivers and canals.
Once you are some distance offshore, you are unlikely to run
aground, and your charts tell you when to start the depth
sounder again. There are no locks. For some time there will
be no land to hit, and at night the lighthouses show you
where it is. The nearest ship will probably not approach
within a mile of you. Best of all, once you are on course, you
do not have to steer by hand; the autopilot will do that for
you, and is probably gallingly better at keeping a course. So
you have, normally, plenty of time to keep a good lookout
and plot your course, even to make tea, and sit in the
Captain's chair while you drink it.

In the canals, unless you are moored, there is no let-up from
driving, one stands most of the time to keep a lookout since
you are close to the banks and other shipping, and the next
lock is coming up soon. In the big rivers you can have a
swingeing current to take account of (just as you have tides at
sea), but with little room to manoeuvre, and there are buoyed
channels that need concentrated navigation. It is very like
driving a car. The Dutch drive their barges all the hours of

daylight, which is a lot of driving, and though we found six hours quite enough in inland waters, we often did more.

We were enjoying the freedom of being at sea. The decks were no longer cluttered with rigging now the masts were up; we looked neater. There was plenty of nice empty sea around, between us and the land, and between *Hosanna* and the nearest ship. It was a refreshing change to see the whole sky, a cloudy bowl above us, instead of patches and glimpses through the trees and buildings. The smell was entirely different, fresh and salty, with a tang of herring, whereas the rivers had at best been new-mown hay and wet leaves, and the canals at worst... we will not go too deeply into the smell of canals at their worst, except to say that drains, slime, chemicals and sugarbeet processing is perhaps the most nauseous combination we came across.

Hosanna dipped and danced on little waves, chuckling, and talking to the seagulls and dolphins. It seemed odd that the cats were not in their respective cupboards, but in their *pension* in France.

We had an excellent three hours, before the fog shut down. As soon as we had crossed the sandbanks we ran into it, thick and white, like sailing through yoghurt. It was the last thing we needed when crossing the intensely busy traffic lanes in the Channel, and it had not been forecast.

As the fog got thicker we ran on radar and tuned in to the Dover Straits control frequency. Ships all over the Straits were reporting their position to identify themselves and to give a visibility report for that position – sometimes it was down to a few cables. We did likewise. It was all impressively efficient, and rather comforting.

Way back in 1947, when Bill had been an assistant Navigator in the big aircraft-carrier HMS *Implacable*, they had been approaching the Dover Straits slowly in very thick fog, with all their radar plot teams closed up in the Operations Room. Though there were officers on the bridge straining eyes and ears through the fog, though there were lookouts on all the four corners of the flight deck, the ship was being conned from the Operations Room with very great care. At that time naval ships were almost the only ones with radar. *Implacable* could see other ships but they would have no idea an aircraft-carrier, then one of the biggest ships afloat, was about to enter the narrow channel. Bill at the age of 20 was in charge of the collision avoidance plot. Another officer controlled the navigational plot, and the senior officer worked on a filter of the two specialist plots, all of which were on tables that had the ship's gyro course and speed automatically fed into them by complex systems of differential gearwheels. There were no computers, only brains.

Bill has to this day no idea what was behind the signal they received at this moment. It was so secret that the ship was never told the background. It was an aircraft ditch alarm in the English Channel and the other side of the straits. *Implacable* was ordered to proceed to that position at full speed.

Her Captain, a phlegmatic man who seldom spoke to anyone under his own rank (you recall the Bostonian rhyme 'where the Cabots speak only to Lowells, and the Lowells speak only to God'. It was a bit like that), ordered the Chief Yeoman to ask the Admiralty to verify the order for full speed, pointing out that the visibility in the straits was about fifty yards. The reply was almost immediate: 'Full speed, repeat full speed'.

The Captain gave the order. The four huge screws made the ship start to shudder as she built her speed up to 34 knots, over 40 miles per hour in the most dangerous and crowded water in the world, where probably no other ship would know we were there, and where there was no way of telling them.

The Captain said to the Ops Room: 'Gentlemen, I do not ask you to increase your vigilance. I know it is already at maximum.' (Captains really did speak like that in those days.) He then removed his monocle, sat in his chair and closed his eyes. He could do no more. His career, his ship, everything aboard was now in the hands of young men half his age, whom he had been responsible for training. He did not interfere. He let his young men do their stuff. There were no separation schemes then to impose one-way traffic in channels. At one point they passed a large ship bound in the opposite direction, at about 200 yards which is less than a ship's length, and they did not see her at all.

After half an hour of this they received a signal to resume their normal course and speed. No explanation. As the Captain gave the order for five knots he said: 'That is not an order to relax, Gentlemen'.

How much easier it is to cope with fog nowadays. Or should be. Despite radar, collision avoidance computers, shore-based traffic control officers monitoring the separation scheme, inter-ship radio – despite all these aids to safety – still ships collide. There are more collisions now with fewer ships under way than there were in the old pre-radar days. What is wrong? The skills of ship-handling are still there; but are they being properly applied? Bill thinks not. HMS *Implacable* had over twenty highly trained officers and plot ratings seeing to her safe navigation; today the officer and rating complement of merchant ships is down very nearly to one man and his dog, and soon, if the ship-owners have their way, the man will go. Good dog, Fido! Seek!

In *Hosanna*, we did not relax. Laurel or Ben 'drove', ie sat in the Captain's chair and kept watch while Bill kept a careful eye on the radar. He also plotted our navigational position using the satellite based Global Positioning System which makes our life much easier these days. We crossed the Dover Straits shipping lanes without any incident, and were relieved to have done so.

We then turned north, in order to keep outside the path of southbound coastal shipping. The fewer ships you encounter in fog the better. This meant that we saw very little as we crossed the Thames Estuary, and up the coast, as we were well offshore.

The fog had lifted soon after midnight, and we began to close the coast. We seemed to be travelling extremely fast, or what passes for fast in our way of life. Suddenly we raised Orford Light, and when we reached it, we would be running off the present chart.

Bill riffled confidently through the drawer looking for the chart of the approaches to Great Yarmouth. He had a nasty shock. It was not there. It's easy to say he should have checked before departure, but he assumed his collection was in good order; it always has been. He normally keeps his charts so, in fact Laurel thinks he is over fussy, and gives them rather more attention than anything else once we are in sea-going mode. Fortunately these waters were his home ground, the only trouble being that he had not sailed them for eight years, and this is perhaps the most constantly changeable part of the British coast, and to encounter shifting sandbanks in the dark of the night without a chart was against all our principles.

He set about making himself a chart. This is not difficult if you know how and have the right publications, but it takes time. Yarmouth harbour lies behind off-lying sandbanks, through which there are few channels, but these are all buoyed. Many of these buoys are lit, and their accurate positions at the time of publication are given in the *List of Lights*, which we had. So he painstakingly set out to construct and draw out his own chart of the area, interpreting the details from the outline that the principal buoys gave him.

This is how it's done. First take a large sheet of paper, and your visual geographic sense. (The latter, unfortunately, cannot be bought at the Boat Show.) Decide on an appropriate scale, then construct a plotting sheet, which is a map with nothing on it except the scales of latitude and longitude. This is not so simple because the scale of longitude changes with latitude, but it can be done geometrically. Then start to plot all the known fixed positions by latitude and longitude, as given in your *List of Lights*. Then read the Admiralty Pilot's description of the coast and the banks, and draw in the outline of what has been described. There have been times when intelligent and discriminating use of a tourist guide has helped here. What you end up with is a useful and workable chart. Is this dodge in the Yachtmaster syllabus we wonder? Given the price of charts and what most yachtsmen can afford, it is a skill that might well be more widely known, as weather sometimes forces the unlucky sailor into harbours he did not plan to visit.

Visibility had improved with nightfall. We had the sails set, and with the wind behind us were making good time. Laurel was enjoying her nightwatch; the last one had been in the Mediterranean approaching Le-Grau-du-Roi in the middle of May. There she had watched the slow passing of the Faraman lighthouse in the Camargue, where, being an extensive nature reserve, there had been few shore lights. Now she could see an almost unbroken string of them punctuated by the clusters of coloured lights that advertised the English seaside.

The first glimmers of dawn began to lighten the sky as we picked up Corton light buoy at four in the morning, and we furled the sails so as to be more manoeuvrable in confined waters. Using Bill's improvised chart, we passed through the Holm channel, navigated accurately to the harbour mouth in spite of the strong cross tide, and passed the pierheads at 0545. We went upstream, passing freighters and coasters and big scarlet oil rig supply ships, and moored on Hall Quay just below Haven Bridge. It was 0615 on Sunday morning. We had done 98 miles from Calais in very good time, with the tide under us a good deal of the journey, a favourable wind, and help from the sails.

We made fast alongside another Dutch barge, which was already alongside the old herring drifter, *Lydia Eva*, which would later be open to visitors. Yarmouth welcomes visitors only if they come by land. Pleasure craft, in our opinion, would be wise to give the place a wide berth; yachts are not part of the plan. It is quite a dangerous harbour, the tide runs fast, and the opening times of Haven Bridge seem capricious. If the Harbour Board could lose their apparent antipathy to yachts and take the trouble to understand what small craft need, and then took some elementary and inexpensive action, such as a pontoon in the summer months, Yarmouth could be as full of Dutch and Belgian yachts as Lowestoft is.

At mid-morning, borne onward by a wild flood tide, we passed through the Haven Bridge in a manner which recalled the after effects of too much syrup of figs. With our small side engine we would have liked to do this at slack water, but the bridge opens only according to the whims of its operators. We had barely got our breath back when we berthed the other side at the quay of Bure Marine Limited whom we had engaged to slip us and do the work on our engines.

We were glad to have arrived. There had been times on our 2295 nautical mile journey, which had begun in earnest in Greece in mid April three months ago, when we had thought we would not make it. It had taken three weeks longer than we planned, but here we were. We threw a quick thanksgiving

Laurel.

to St Nicholas. He is the most popular saint among Greek sea-farers and a large proportion of the smaller boats in Greece are named after him. His ikon is often to be found on board, and they take it out on deck when the weather turns rough. He is expected to moderate the weather, or get wet too. And serve him right. It was somehow right that the patron saint of our destination should have such a strong link with our starting point, and the medieval church of St Nicholas in Great Yarmouth stands at the head of the market place; we could see its tower over the rooftops on the opposite bank.

Our daughter Shelley, and granddaughter Jennifer, had arrived from Hertfordshire by midday, and we celebrated. We had a wonderful late Sunday lunch, Bill having managed to buy a rib roast and some strawberries even though it was Sunday. The day was warm and cloudless, and we all ate on the verandah. In the evening Ben and Claire got a lift home with Shelley, and were in good order to go to work the following day, as they had hoped. We were glad that the whole weekend operation had gone so well. Trips at sea do not always go according to plan, and many a weekend yachtsman is late at his desk on Monday morning after a night of battling with the tides.

We do not propose to go into the detail of the weeks we spent in the boatyard. We had missed our turn on the slip. No matter how friendly the staff, nor how good at their job, they had other clients beside us. The delay was not unreasonable but very irritating.

Being late also ran us into the British summer holiday period. This meant that, though the engines had been ordered well in advance, delivery of some of the parts we needed was delayed. This is an appalling indictment of the efficiency of British industry in the last day of the twentieth century. Stocks could be maintained, even if the workers who make them need their holidays. We are proud to be English, and we do not like to have to buy foreign because British firms cannot deliver items that are in their catalogues but cannot be found on their shelves. Other things did not go our way either. The galvanising tank in Barrack Road was being enlarged and would not be doing business for a month.

One of the bright patches in our quilt was seeing the children often, and a spell of lovely summer weather. We bought an elderly Mini and a shoe-horn to get Bill into it, and did some visiting.

Our plan had been to finish our refit and leave Yarmouth in mid-August, to make our way easily down to the South coast where we had a date at the Southampton Boat Show in September, preceded by a Club weekend rally at Beaulieu.

It was a fortnight before anything happened at all, then we were moved alongside the quay where the crane could reach us. In preparation for work starting we took up the movable wooden floor of the verandah to protect it from oil and scratches, and unbolted the huge steel hatch beneath it which covers the engine room. A corresponding hatch in the roof was also removed. With the floor gone the verandah became a huge pit that you could look down into, as Dante gazed down into Hell, and into which the boatyard crane probed and groped and began to remove things as if they were bad teeth.

The dead Cummins went, wet liners and all. While we were there, a survey vessel came into the yard with engine trouble; she had Cummins engines too, and her wet liners had corroded as well. We cried together with her owner: 'This shouldn't happen to a cheap engine, let alone a very expensive one'.

The generator went to Ipswich for a factory renovation and came back in a worse state than it went, like humans going to hospital. We put the generator forward into the forepeak to make room for a new one. Other unsatisfactory bits were extracted. All of them spilt oil and rust and dirty water over our boat. Our decks became filthy, and we laid plastic down in the wheelhouse in a desperate but unsuccessful attempt to stop it tracking indoors.

Then we sat with our black gaping hole open, waiting, as it were for the dentist, in the shape of engineers. Another fortnight followed, during which the few things that could be done off the slip were done, and increasing exasperation set in. The rest had to wait until the day when finally *Hosanna* lurched and graunched up the slip, and the real work began.

Not one but two new engines were to go in. We kept the trusty wing engine that had alone brought us all the way from

Lyon, and were adding two more, centre and starboard. We weren't going to get caught like *that* again. Though the engines had not yet arrived, much work had to be done first and it could only be done on the slip. Holes were cut in the hull for new shafts. There were hold-ups and misfits and further delays, including extra-high tides which sometimes prevented work on the new shafts and propellers. Ben arrived to help with antifouling the bottom, which all of us joined in.

At the end of August we pointed out to the yard that we should have been finished two weeks ago and that we were determined to leave before another week was gone, come what may. Our rally was the weekend of 10 September. Things began to get a bit frantic. An entire football team seemed to be working on the boat: Laurel fell over them everywhere, even in her galley. They were welding, pipe running, greasing, hammering, antifouling (when the tide allowed), aligning, maligning, and losing their cool, their tools and their tempers. Bill hurtled from one query to another with increasingly inventive language and his mouth in a straight line. Laurel dashed between antifouling and clearing up welding slag, and her own personal fight against bootmarks.

On 1 September we went back in the water, not without difficulty as one of the wires that controlled the downhaul of the slip had parted. Nevertheless, the yard used their collective imagination and got us in the water in a series of sticky lurches which knocked more books off the shelves than any of our sea passages. Someone was still welding engine beds while we did so. Then at last the new engines went in. The football team redoubled its efforts. Laurel gave up the fight against filth and went shopping every day. Among other things we got ourselves a mobile phone.

On Monday 5 September we declared our intention of going next day, as the good weather did not look as if it would hold up much longer. Half the football team had worked all Sunday. Now we were still waiting for the finishing touches, were still filthy and disorganised with only a few days before our rally, and no time to paint ship before the Boat Show opened. We were anxious to leave, but distressed at the condition we were in.

On Tuesday we realised that too many important things were still unfinished and that we would be foolish to go. Laurel spent hours in the engine room patiently greasing the new shafts, 21 potsful of grease for each shaft, and each pot (about a coffee mugful) took 20 minutes to screw down with a brass wingnut, like administering a hypodermic of treacle to a rhinoceros.

On Wednesday we left. We were up at six to be greeted by thick fog. Men were still working on board. Laurel was screwing down the last of the greasepots in the engine room. A hydraulic leak was traced and fixed. By mid-morning the fog lifted, and at 1345 we flushed out the last shipwright but one, and cast off. Whether Dick had purposely stayed with us to see us safely under the two o'clock bridge was not clear, but offloading him afterwards with a vicious ebb under us was not easy: after two attempts we began to think he would have to come to Southampton with us. Then he managed to grab a ladder that we pointed him at, and the ebb-tide flushed us out to sea almost before we could wave him goodbye.

The weather forecast had been dubious. It was for south or south-west winds force three to four increasing to five. In normal circumstances Bill would not have taken a chance with a freshening head wind. He worked out that, with our new engine power, we should be approaching the Straits of Dover, and thus have a weather shore to shelter us a bit before the wind reached a strength that would worry us. The long range forecast was predicting gales by the weekend. There would be no second chance to get south before the Boat Show.

In other respects too, we were foolish, because we were still securing loose gear for sea after our departure. After being in the yard for so many weeks, many items were not in their proper places, nor were they secured for sea.

Everything went well for about eight hours, as Bill had expected. Comforting quantities of Irish stew had stayed our stomachs. The new engines were donkeying away, with a reas-suring rumble. Then the wind increased rather more suddenly than seemed likely. By midnight it was blowing force six from the south-east, and we had to ease speed as we were beginning to pound hard into a short, sharp sea. Something blew off the roof in a gust. 'What was that?' said Bill, scarcely sleeping. Laurel peered into the flying spray. 'It's the verandah floor,' she said. We had not had time to replace the two wooden sections, which had been lashed to the roof. Or so we thought: now they were floating in the sea behind us. 'Shall we go back for them?' We sometimes do this sort of thing for man overboard drill. 'Not on your Nelly,' said Laurel shortly. No one likes to take unnecessary risks in rough weather. She was not enjoying this passage. With every slam the heart pounds a little, even if you know your boat is strong and seaworthy. The mouth gets dry and you swallow a lot. You try not to sound shrewish and fretful when you make a suggestion, an octave above and tens of decibels louder than your normal speech pattern. Above all, you concentrate on what you are doing, driving the ship and watching out for other craft, which helps enormously, but does not quite prevent the pit of the stomach lurching.

The ebbtide turned to flood and we now had wind against tide. The slamming and pounding became worse as the seas became steeper. The wind had increased to force six, and with a wave height of about two metres it was getting dangerous. At 0200 Bill eased speed to slow ahead which helped the comfort, but every now and then *Hosanna* got out of sympathy with the sea and a violent bang would shake us from end to end. Bits of boat, mats, and buckets that we had neglected to secure properly swished past the wheelhouse and disappeared northward, noisily reproachful as they passed.

We were east of the Kentish Knock just before five in the morning. Laurel was on watch and Bill was asleep when the big bang came. It sounded like an explosion. Laurel didn't need to wake him. It was a moonless night and at first it was impossible to see through the spray what had happened; it clearly was not a typical slam into a wave, and we thought at first we might have hit some wreckage, or even, dear God, a floating container. The ship was making no real headway, but she hadn't been doing that for some time. In reality we suppose it took only seconds to realise that our foremast was not there anymore. It is amazing how in crises the quality of time changes and one thinks and perceives in slow time. Ten minutes takes an hour to pass.

The first and most important thing, after strong words to one's stomach about the Irish stew, and a recommendation to one's heart to get out of one's mouth and back to its proper place, was to stop engines in case any ropes had gone over the side. These might get tangled in the propellers and so disable us. Bill made a quick and immediate foray forward to assess the situation. 'We're very lucky, really,' he reported as he made the safety of the wheelhouse once more. 'I think I can get it all inboard and out of harm's way'. 'Do you need me?' asked Laurel. 'No. Stay here and keep the boat head to wind, or as comfortable as you can. The fewer jerks the better.'

Dry mouthed, Laurel watched as he departed forward again, wearing his safety harness this time. He took with him bolt-cutters and an axe.

When some calamity occurs at sea, the interdependence of the crew, especially if there are only two of you, is something almost unknown to landsmen. Each of you has a part to play, each depends on the other for their lives, each is sharply aware of the dangers. In this case it was Bill who was running the risk of going overboard, and Laurel blessed, not for the first time, the foresight that had caused him to install stout steel guardrails all along the bulwarks, for the benefit, oddly enough, of her dodgy hip. He was now reaping the reward, clipping his safety harness to something strong. By that same token however, the guardrails themselves were stout enough to cause severe injury if a limb got pinned between them and a rolling rogue section of mast before it was lashed and immovable. Laurel alerted Heaven to the whole problem, and prayed earnestly but briefly for a satisfactory outcome. She, too, was busy at her task of conning the ship, and would only be in physical danger if Bill failed in his.

Going slow ahead on one engine, she conned in such a way as to keep the ship's head just off the wind, thus the side Bill was working on had a very slight lee, but the ship, being almost head on to the waves, would not roll. Pitching did not matter so much.

We had had very little sail set at the time. Wherever the first fracture had been, by the time the mast hit the deck it had fallen into three lengths of about 3 metres each, leaving a short stump sticking up from the tabernacle. The foresprit, a spar of about 12 metres, had fallen by good chance between the main-stay and the roller gear of the mainstaysail, a little of which had been set. The sprit was firmly held; otherwise it could have been a formidable weapon sweeping from side to side like a gigantic scythe. The masthead section of the foremast was over the starboard side, but was held by the rigging and was being towed along close to the hull, banging and crashing and busily destroying the paintwork. Its roller furling gear was substantially intact, but the two other broken pieces, both with rigging attached, were rolling about the deck like a pair of steamrollers dancing the rumba.

Bill hauled inboard all loose rope first, and made it fast. It was still blowing hard, with gusts over thirty knots, and the sea was sweeping every few seconds over our comparatively low decks which made standing difficult enough, let alone lift-ing and working. One hand for yourself and one for the ship is the traditional sailor's working rule, but it has to be broken now and then. Like then. Thank God for safety belts, and a strong point to attach them to: the second requirement being all too often forgotten on some of today's production yachts.

He caught, and lashed into the scuppers, first the larger of the two loose sections which could have broken his legs if he hadn't been quick enough to jump over it. There was plenty of loose rope about to do the lashing. If there is one thing that characterises the boats we own, it is miles of string up the masts. (Well, about one mile actually, spread over all the three masts.)

The smaller portion on deck was more easily driven into a corner like an angry pig, and fastened to the windlass. That left the masthead portion, weighing about 120 kilos, dangling in the water. It was impossible to untangle the 12 mm diameter wires, so he cut them, leaving the mast on only one rope halyard.

He asked Laurel – which in itself was no easy matter, the instructions having to be shouted over the wind – to bear away and take the ship's head off the wind so the boat would start to roll. Laurel did so and Bill waited for a moment as the rolling increased, and until the boat rolled the right way at the right time and by the right amount. As the floating mast section rose up the ship's side, he lifted to help it and the mast flopped over the solid steel guardrails and reposed neatly in the scuppers. This was a trick he had learned from the Skipper, as we called his father, who used the rolling motion of his herring drifter to get the nets in more easily.

Bill held on while Laurel brought the boat's head back into the wind and then he lashed the mast to the strong guardrail stanchions. It was only half an hour since the breaking of the mast. He came back and demanded praise and coffee. He got both. Relief welled up in both of us, and Laurel's shaking hands caused the teaspoon to tinkle a tattoo against the coffee mug as she spooned in plenty of sugar to counteract the abating panic.

We now had to make decisions as we drank the coffee. Bill was very nearly exhausted. One has to concentrate very hard to make good decisions in that condition, otherwise one ends up making a series of mistakes that can, at sea, just as on a motorway, lead to one's death. He sat still in the darkness breathing deeply, his weak lungs taking time to give him his breath back. Then, while we motored at slow ahead into the seas, he started to think aloud so as to bring Laurel into the decision-making.

Clearly getting *Hosanna* to the Boat Show was now out of the question. The latest weather forecast had the wind continuing to veer to the south-west and strengthening further, so even if we had been still fully masted, a continuation down-Channel to Southampton would have been unwise. In the circumstances, damaged and tired, we had three options.

The first was to heave to where we were; that is to manoeuvre the boat so that she makes the minimum way through the water, stays roughly where she is. What! In the middle of one of the busiest traffic lanes in the world? That didn't seem like a very good idea.

The second was to turn and head for Harwich which we had already passed, and which lay now in a roughly north-north-westerly direction. Harwich is a deep water port into which we could navigate without danger even in rough sea. But that rough sea, getting rougher with every gust of wind, was the fount of all our troubles. We were by now all too aware of our lack of prudence in leaving harbour in a hurry, without properly securing the deck gear, let alone our domestic treasures. Barges roll when beam on to waves; dear God, how they roll! It is their weak point from a sea-keeping point of view, and even the short time while we turned would probably give us at least one very bad roll which could cause further damage.

Had we, for instance lost the foremast because of an inherent weakness, as we supposed? Or had Bill erred in setting up the rigging to the right tension, and if so, what about the mainmast which would fall above our heads if it gave way? And even then, if we managed to turn without rolling too much, Bill knew that we would be running before the wind under power with a substantial following sea. The wavelength we could now observe was just short of the ship's length, and it would make her pitch so as to lift her propellers out of the water each time the stern rose, causing the engines to race dangerously.

Our sail setting capability was severely curtailed by the loss of the foremast, and the fallen foresprit jamming the gear on the mainmast. It is possible that with concentration and skill Bill could have handled *Hosanna*, easing speed to the right degree, and playing the engine throttles, but he was already nearly worn out; and we judged it better that he should keep some reserve of energy and concentration, just in case.

The third option was to continue stemming the wind and sea, and make slow progress towards the weather shore. If we edged over to the westward, we could be more comfortable by finding a partial lee behind some of the Thames Estuary sand banks which are near the surface or dry at low water. If the wind stayed south, we would probably make Ramsgate, but if not we would enter the estuary and try for the Medway.

Bill also reasoned that Harwich was to leeward, and that his tiredness was conducive to mistakes, and a mistake off a lee-shore gives one little time to recover. It was evidently not our lucky year. Not that he is superstitious; just careful.

So he felt that the latter course, to head southward, was the better, even though it would take longer before we got to

148

shelter. Carried unanimously. Over the years, by conscientiously consulting Laurel on all decisions of this nature, Bill has taught her a lot about what he calls 'route planning', a vital subject for sailing boats. It also helps to have two minds reviewing the factors affecting the decision.

It had not occurred to us to radio for assistance. Bill sometimes says that radios should be forbidden to yachtsmen in their first few years at sea, so as to teach them to manage on their own. He has no time for the racing fleets that expect the whole world to go to their assistance if unseaworthy gear gives way or they lose the tin opener. His family have been lifeboat crew for generations. Of course, one would risk one's life to save idiots if push came to shove, but it gives one an odd perspective on rescue if the disaster is caused by what amounts to lunatic carelessness. At least if we were lunatics we were not asking anyone else to join in.

Nevertheless, with leisure to consider what was next on the agenda, and with confidence creeping back as we passed mile after slow and painful mile towards safety, we began to think of whom we should inform of our change of plan. Daughter first. She was planning to meet us. So we used our new digital phone and it worked splendidly out there in the North Sea. This conjures up very strange thoughts: a sailor pausing to phone his solicitor while getting into his liferaft: 'How are you? Fine. Well no, actually, I'm drowning. Can I make a quick will?'

Daughter was a bit squeaky to start with, but she could hear that we were both all right, and by now in reasonable spirits.

We realised that no one else would welcome a call in the middle of the night so our uncustomary radio verbosity had to be curbed.

There had been publicity arranged for our arrival at Southampton. We had to cancel all that, and we passed a telephone message to that effect later in the forenoon, giving our expected time of arrival at Ramsgate.

It was midday as we rounded the breakwater in rough seas and found a reception party of TV cameras filming us entering Ramsgate. Somewhat hairy it all looked, with our snapped off foremast stump pointing this way and that as we rolled, and the spray flying over the boat. Real Captain Ahab stuff. We looked battered and filthy (the boat that is) but they were not to know that this was due to the Bure Marine football team and not the seas off Kentish Knock.

We were only two pensioners on board *Hosanna*, but we had coped with our mishap without injury to ourselves and made harbour without assistance. We felt good about this, because a few hours after and not far away, the fifty foot sloop *Ingotism* belonging to the Bank of England Sailing Club was dismasted with eighty healthy athletic young men on board, four of whom were Yachtmasters. They put out a distress call, and had to be helped back to safety.

Active life does not stop at pensiontide. Old dogs may find it hard to learn new tricks, but they have plenty of experience with the old ones. Calling for assistance did not occur to us, even though the shock after the event left Laurel shaking and Bill seriously tired after his solo work on the foredeck. Nor should it have done, if nothing else was amiss. Dismasting is not all that rare, though it ought to be rarer still. It had happened to Bill once before in about 1967, in almost exactly the same place, and then the ocean-racing crew of six had rigged a jury mast and sailed themselves into Harwich. That had been a wooden mast too. Do plastic boats breed plastic crews?

As we rocked gently in Ramsgate harbour, we counted our blessings. We listened to the gale that roared outside, and got reports from the Beaulieu Rally we had been unable to attend. 'The weather's foul!' they screamed down our mobile phone. 'Nobody's come. You're missing nothing.'

All hurry was at an end. From now on, we would return gratefully to softly, softly as a way of life. As worried children came down to check up on us, and we received offers of help from friends, we got the damage sorted out. We went to the Boat Show by Mini.

Revelling in the snail pace. Life back to walking speed. Slow is beautiful. Back to normal except for the oily footfalls on our deck still resisting scouring powder and elbow grease.

Then we got two calls on our mobile phone.

'Stir your stumps, Captain,' said Laurel. 'That was my brother in Australia. Can he come cruising in three days time?

And the other was from Gwen and Valerie in France. They want to go on holiday in a week's time: can we come and collect our cats?'

Bill sighed and put on his overalls. Laurel went to the fore-peak to look for the white paint. We paused for a moment to listen to the weather forecast. Here we go again. One journey ends, another begins. We would have been astonished if we could have foreseen where the next would take us.

APPENDIX 1

Plan of Hosanna

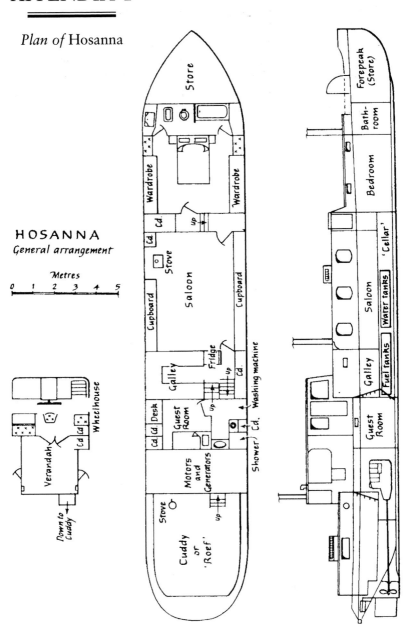

HOSANNA
General arrangement

Metres
0   1   2   3   4   5

INDEX

Index